THE

Honeysuckle

COOKBOOK

THE
Honeysuckle
COOKBOOK

100 Healthy, Feel-Good Recipes
to Live Deliciously

DZUNG LEWIS

with Jess Thomson
Photographs by Eva Kolenko

RODALE
New York

To Bà Ngoại and Ba

CONTENTS

INTRODUCTION

I was born and raised in Santa Clara, California. My parents were Vietnamese immigrants, and our house was always filled with the aroma of food cooking. My sister and I were usually assigned tasks in the kitchen; it was my parents' way of keeping two rambunctious little girls occupied on weekends when we didn't have homework or school activities. My grandmother also lived with us throughout much of my childhood. She came of age in French-accented Saigon, Vietnam, and her influence and presence played a big role in my early culinary development. I was exposed to a combination of French classics (think duck à l'orange) and Vietnamese staples (i.e., clay pot caramelized catfish). Together we watched television chefs Jacques Pépin and Martin Yan, and I soon began dreaming of a life devoted to creating delicious meals to share with people in an inviting, loving way. Among the first dishes I cooked, around age eight or nine, were simple ones like Tomatoes Provençale (page 184) and Mom's Famous Flan (page 223). In seventh grade, I began cooking family meals, often asking my dad, who also loved being in the kitchen, to seek out ingredients for me well before I could drive myself to the store. When my dad cooked, I was there by his side, learning how everyday Vietnamese dishes like Lemongrass Chicken Stir-Fry (Gà Xào Sả Ớt, page 131) come together.

Throughout college in Santa Clara, I worked as a server in a few restaurants, and I always enjoyed watching and learning how the chefs played with flavor. The restaurant work made me curious about attending culinary school, but coming from an academics-first Asian-American household, my parents guided me toward a more "stable" and prestigious career in corporate America. They didn't want to see me "labor" like they did to make ends meet. So, I ended up graduating college with a business degree in finance, a total last-possible-minute decision, and probably the most polar opposite of my passion. I didn't want to be stuck in a cubicle, so I continued working in restaurants on the side (for fun). Even though finance wasn't the most ideal career for me, I'm thankful for the business experience I gained.

Still, when I progressed into a full-time job as a financial analyst in the Bay Area, I couldn't help but notice the lack of creativity and stimulation that I naturally craved from a career. I had zero passion for crunching numbers all day long (and some weekends and holidays, too). Often, to flex my creative muscles, I began baking in earnest after work, starting by making my way through all of *The Complete Magnolia Bakery Cookbook*. (My coworkers loved me for bringing in all the goodies.) This was all-new territory for me because I'd grown up baking only from boxed mixes. Baking from scratch was an interesting daily challenge and led me to discover new techniques and flavors—and I found so much inspiration from cookbooks and television cooking shows. Eventually, I even took on a weekend gig at Sur la Table, the cookware store, as an assistant where I would prep all the ingredients before students arrived for cooking classes. While most other assistants dreaded the mundane labor of chopping vegetables and carefully measuring items, I found it gave me a level of peace. It became my way to escape the more banal confines of a gray cubicle. I loved the energetic environment

of the kitchen, and the proximity to food—it gave me new life.

Fast-forward a few years to when I met Nate, now my husband, who tried to charm me with what he refers to as his "culinary genius." (You'll learn more about that later.) He also happens to be half-Korean, which was definitely a plus because I love Korean food! Through him, I inherited a new family of flavors and culture, and Korean food has become a mainstay in my dietary repertoire. Nate also encouraged me to start the *Honeysuckle* YouTube channel as a way to find my voice through food. Now after ten years of uploading a video or two a week, and nearly six hundred cooking videos about everything from baking to easy weeknight meals, I've finally understood how truly varied my background is. I am immersed in an American and Californian melting pot where cultures from all corners are somehow mixed in new ways. I consider myself lucky to have been exposed to everything from authentic Mexican flavors to exotic Burmese cuisine, from Ethiopian spreads to Pakistani dishes. And especially now, living in Los Angeles, where the culinary rules always seem to be rewritten, I am continually motivated to play and experiment with flavors. So I might heighten the umami character of a good marinara with a splash of fish sauce—a trick my dad relied on—or amp up the flavor of an ordinary quick bread with Japanese matcha powder. If you watch my YouTube videos, you already know that I call these little tweaks my "Honeysuckle twists."

As my interest in cooking and experimenting grew, so did our family. We now are raising two young children (and a curious border collie) with growing appetites. Our oldest, Erisy, has developed into a little foodie herself, with discerning taste buds and strong opinions. (She does *not* tolerate leftovers.) With each new phase in life, my culinary interests are always expanding, and for everything that food has taught me, my goal is to share that knowledge and inspiration with all of you. This has always been the point of my cooking channel: to create a place to interact with other food lovers and build a community, so I can also draw inspiration from viewers' unique perspectives. That community has been the biggest catalyst in my development as a cook and really encouraged me to follow my dream of creating a cookbook. So here it is: *The Honeysuckle Cookbook*. It's a compilation of some of my family's best Vietnamese recipes, plenty of easy, everyday meals with those Honeysuckle twists, and a few time-tested favorites from the *Honeysuckle* channel I know you wouldn't let me leave out, like the beloved Cold Buster Tea (page 22) and Quicker Beef Pho (page 91). Since I'm a busy mom, I know a mix of fast, delicious, and healthy options that can be whipped up on a weeknight is needed. You'll find lots of those but also a few longer projects for weekends or holidays, when you might have a bit more time in the kitchen. I hope this inspires you to cook and then to share what you make with your family and friends. Enjoy!

IN DZUNG'S KITCHEN

Every time I publish a video on *Honeysuckle*, I receive so many questions about my kitchen—my audience wants to know what ingredients I always have on hand, and what tools I like best. Below are the things I can't live without in both my fridge and pantry, and a list of the tools that I need in my kitchen. Some of them are investments, but they're definitely worth the money if they are high-quality and durable.

DZUNG'S KITCHEN STAPLES

Alternative milks: While we usually have cow's milk in the fridge, I like to have almond, oat, and soy milks also. Explore them to find out what you like best in coffee drinks and tea!

Avocado oil: Made with heart-healthy avocado, avocado oil has a mild flavor perfectly suited to the big, bold flavors of Asian food, and it also holds up well to heat. I use this as my everyday cooking oil.

Broths: I always have broth on hand for soups and sauces. When I use chicken and beef broths, I choose low-sodium broths, so that I can control the saltiness of the final product myself.

Chili-garlic sauce: Chili-garlic sauce is a delicious, spicy store-bought blend of chiles, garlic, and other flavorings, stirred into a spoonable sauce (but not pureed like sriracha).

Cider vinegar: Also known as apple cider vinegar, this is a tangy favorite I always have for salad dressings and vinaigrettes.

Citrus: Lemons, limes, and oranges are great, easy ways to add flavor to food. I keep them in the fridge for freshness.

Coconut milk: Look for full-fat coconut milk in cans or coconut milk beverage in cartons, and pay attention to which one the recipe calls for. For beverages and lighter sauces, I usually use the kind in the carton. If you use canned coconut milk, be sure to shake the can before opening so that the fat that sometimes floats to the top of the can during storage gets mixed back in!

Curry powder: Made with a blend of dried spices that differs based on both the brand of spice you're buying and the region of the curry blend, curry powders can vary widely. I typically purchase "Madras curry powder," made based on the flavors from the Madras region of India, but use one you like.

Fish sauce: Used mostly as a flavor enhancer, fish sauce is a crucial ingredient in Southeast Asian cuisine—so don't be tempted to skip it. Yes, it's made from fermented fish, but think of it as something that adds umami. Use it in the fish sauce vinaigrette on page 112!

Garlic: I always keep a few bulbs on hand! Store them at room temperature. I also usually have a jar of preminced garlic in the refrigerator, because it's an easy shortcut when I'm pressed for time.

Ginger: I always have ginger in the produce drawer of my refrigerator. Look for ginger with no visible damp or colored spots; the skin should be smooth and taut. Peel it before using.

Gochugaru: These are Korean chile flakes, made from Korean chiles, which are slightly sweeter and almost smoky when dried. I buy the coarse-ground kind at an Asian market or in the Asian section of a large grocery store. The flakes are bigger than the texture of other chile powders, and they are cut into flat shards, so they almost sparkle! Invest in a big bag, and it will last a long time if you store it in the fridge or freezer for freshness. Red pepper flakes don't have the same flavor.

Gochujang: Gochujang is a fermented seedless Korean chile paste, made with Korean chiles,

sugar, and sometimes other flavorings. It's great for marinades, sauces, and soups that need a little kick with a side of sweetness.

Herbs: I always have fresh herbs like cilantro, parsley, and basil in my fridge. To store herbs with soft green stems, cut a fresh end on the stems immediately when you get them home. Wrap the ends in damp paper towels, or put them in a jar with water as you would for flowers, and store them on the counter or in the fridge. They last longer this way.

Hoisin sauce: Hoisin is a soy-based sauce that's thick, sweet, and salty—which makes it the perfect addition to marinades and sauces.

Kimchi: Kimchi is actually a group of fermented foods in Korea, but in the US, it most commonly refers to the spicy Korean napa cabbage version. Although recipes vary widely, it's usually made by coating salted cabbage with a mixture of ground chiles, Korean pears, onion, garlic, ginger, and fish sauce and allowing it to ferment. The longer it sits in your fridge, the stronger and more savory it gets!

Korean soup soy sauce (*guk ganjang*)**:** Stronger and richer in flavor that traditional soy sauce, Korean soup soy sauce is the by-product of making *doenjang*, which is Korean fermented soybean paste. Look for it in the Korean soy sauce section of any large Asian grocery store.

Matcha powder: Matcha powder is a bright green powder that dissolves in water to make a tea called matcha, and is made from the finely ground leaves of whole-leaf green tea. It can vary widely in price; fancy matchas are extremely expensive. Because we're using it for blended drinks, baking, and desserts, you can purchase a more moderately priced tea for these recipes.

Neutral oil: When I use oil for cooking, I like using something that doesn't add too much extra flavor, so foods don't taste heavy. Avocado oil is perfect, but any neutral oil with a high smoke point will work, such as grapeseed oil, peanut oil, or ghee.

Olive oil: When I use olive oil, I use extra-virgin olive oil, because I prefer the flavor. You don't need to spend a fortune, but look for the extra-virgin label. Olive oil is great for using in dressing and sauces.

Oyster sauce: Made from cooked oysters, this rich, savory sauce doesn't actually taste super fishy—and it's a great addition to sauces and condiments. Because it's often thickened with cornstarch, it gives sauces body and adds silkiness.

Panko bread crumbs: Japanese bread crumbs, or panko, are flat, lightweight crumbs made from airy white bread. They add more texture than regular bread crumbs, making for crispier fried foods. They also do a great job binding things like meatballs and meat loaf together.

Rice: I like to use short-grain Calrose rice because I prefer the texture, which is somewhere between jasmine and sushi rice, but you can try different varietals to see what you like best. Always rinse rice before cooking it to rid the grains of any excess starch. (See Flawlessly Cooked Rice, page 192, for more information.)

Rice noodles: Rice noodles are just that—noodles made out of rice. They come fresh or dried, and in a wide variety of shapes and thicknesses. For more information, see Rice Noodle Tips (page 113).

Rice paper rounds (*bánh tráng*)**:** Rice paper rounds are the wrappers for the spring rolls on page 181. They're basically wide, flat noodles, but so thin that a quick dip in warm water makes them pliable. Handle them carefully; they're quite brittle when dry.

Rice vinegar: Milder and sweeter than most vinegars, rice vinegar is used in many Asian cuisines.

Salt: Salt amps up the other flavors in any given recipe. I use Diamond Crystal kosher salt for everyday cooking and baking. I prefer kosher salt because it is less salty than table salt and it enhances the flavor of food instead of just making it salty.

Sambal oelek: Sambal oelek is a chunky Indonesian chile paste made from fresh chiles and usually nothing else—so it has a brighter, spicier flavor than a typical chili-garlic paste. Sometimes it's also made with vinegar, which makes it a bit sharper as well. It has visible chile seeds and is increasingly available in American grocery stores.

Scallions: Also called green onions, these are a staple in so many Asian cuisines—including Vietnamese food. I prefer using just the green and light green portions after cutting off (and discarding) the white ends.

Sesame oil (toasted): This oil lends its signature rich and nutty flavor to many Korean, Japanese, and Chinese dishes, like my Veggie Mu Shu (page 148) or Korean Braised Short Ribs (page 165). The toasted version yields better flavor than the kind not labeled "toasted," and a little goes a long way. I like the Kadoya brand.

Sesame seeds: Look for plain white seeds, toasted white seeds, and black sesame seeds, and experiment with their flavors. They add a great nutty flavor and crunch to noodles and sauces—and just about anything else you want!

Shallots: Shallots are smaller purple members of the onion family, with a milder flavor than regular onions. In Vietnamese cuisine, they're often fried as a condiment or garnish (see Fried Shallots, page 201).

Soy sauce: It's a staple of many Asian cuisines, and I use it in many of the recipes in this book. Regular or reduced-sodium soy sauce will work

in these recipes. I usually purchase the reduced-sodium kind.

Spices: I find many dried spices, like onion powder, garlic powder, cumin, chili powder, and various dried herbs, are a super convenient way to add flavor without always having to have fresh ingredients on hand. Store them in a cool, dry place, and purchase them in small quantities if you can, because they will lose flavor over time.

Sriracha: Yes, that red bottle with the green cap. Sriracha is a fermented chile-garlic condiment that adds just the right amount of spice to sauces, and a punchy seasoning for everything else. (Try it in Nate's Turkey Meatballs, page 160!) Don't confuse it with chili-garlic *sauce*, which is a chunkier mixture.

Ssamjang: *Ssamjang* is a Korean dipping sauce made with *doenjang* (Korean fermented soybean paste), gochujang (Korean chile paste), sesame oil, garlic, onions, and sometimes sugar. You can make it yourself, but I find the premade ones convenient and delicious—and perfect for the steaks on page 135. Look for it near the gochujang at any Asian market.

Sweetened condensed milk: Always at the bottom of every Vietnamese coffee, a layer of sweetened condensed milk will give it just the right amount of sweetness. It's milk that's been condensed—all the water is taken out—and then sweetened, so a little goes a long way for the drinks in the first chapter. Use your own palate as a guide and add more to taste when you use it.

Tamarind: Tamarind is a delicious sour fruit that grows in pods on a tree in Southeast Asia. The insides of the pods are made into pulp, which can be purchased dried and used to make a paste for cooking (see DIY Tamarind Paste, page 97), where it adds a tangy, bright flavor. Look for tamarind pulp in blocks wrapped in plastic. You can also purchase tamarind concentrate, which I use in the

Tamarind-Cumin Grilled Pork Chops (page 151). It has a similar consistency to honey, except it's a darker brown color. You'll find the concentrate more easily, but the block can be found at any Asian market.

Vietnamese coffee: Look for brands such as Café du Monde or Trung Nguyên, which are preground to the perfect consistency for use in a Vietnamese coffee filter.

DZUNG'S KITCHEN TOOLS

Baking pans: I have a variety of pans for baking, but the ones I use most are my pie pan, my 8-inch cake pans, and a 9-inch tart pan.

Baking sheets: Sturdy, heavy rimmed baking sheets cook more evenly than cheaper baking sheets and they'll last much longer. Look for half baking sheets that measure 18 × 13 inches. It's great to have two.

Blender: I use a heavy-duty blender for sauces and soups, but even a modest blender works well—it just won't be as thorough when chopping frozen vegetables or ice.

Cast-iron skillet: My 10-inch cast-iron skillet is my kitchen's workhorse. When you purchase one, make sure you season it well before using. I have a YouTube video with step-by-step instructions detailing just how I like to do this!

Dutch oven: A sturdy, heavy cooking vessel (I love Le Creuset) is crucial for soups and stews. It seems expensive, but a good one should last a lifetime. Look for at least a 3.5-quart capacity.

Immersion blender: An immersion blender (or stick blender) is a small machine with a submersible blending attachment on one end. It can be used to puree soups or to froth steamed milk.

Knives: Like all good cookware, the right knives can last a lifetime. My staples are a chef's knife, a small paring knife, and a serrated knife for breads. I like Material Kitchen, Wüstof, Henckels, or Shun brands. Expect to spend upward of $75 on a good chef's knife! It can last you a lifetime if you sharpen it properly and take care of it—never put your knives in a dishwasher.

Mandoline: I use a mandoline to thinly slice vegetables and meats. It's not something I think everyone needs to own—especially if you're confident in your knife skills—but if you get one, make sure it's a good brand (such as Benriner).

Mason jars: Because they're useful and inexpensive, mason jars are everywhere in my house! I use them for breakfast on the go (see Overnight Oats Four Ways, page 45), for storing leftovers, and for blending sauces and dressings.

Microplane: A Microplane is a long, handled tool for grating ginger, garlic, citrus zest, and cheese into very fine shreds.

Multipot: Sold under many different brand names, multipots are appliances that can perform many different functions; for the recipes in this book, you'll need one that can both slow-cook and pressure-cook. See Getting to Know Your Multipot (page 157) for more info.

Nonstick skillet: It's great to have a nonstick skillet for searing meat and making egg dishes, but make sure its coating doesn't contain any harmful materials (such as Teflon).

Ramekins: These small 4- or 6-ounce round baking dishes are great for desserts and snacks, and also convenient when you're prepping ingredients.

Vietnamese coffee filter: Vietnamese coffee is made in a four-piece filter setup also known as a phin. See Finding and Brewing Vietnamese Coffee (page 24) for more information.

morning rituals must include COFFEE & TEA!

When I finally manage to make it downstairs in the mornings, nothing can get rolling until I start sipping a steaming-hot, delicious latte. Or depending on how the night went (remember, two little kids?), a strong coffee like my Vietnamese Shakerato (page 26) or, if necessary, a cold-busting citrus tea that heals from the inside out. Whatever you're facing in the morning, here are several of my favorite cups of relief to start the day right.

VALENCIA LATTE

MAKES 1 large latte   **TIME** 10 minutes

2 (3-inch) strips orange zest

3 tablespoons ground Vietnamese coffee (or 2 shots espresso)

Boiling water

1 teaspoon sugar

½ teaspoon vanilla extract

1 cup milk of your choice plus 2 tablespoons canned coconut milk, steamed together (see Steaming Milk below)

There's a coffee shop I used to visit in Santa Clara called Voyager Craft Coffee. I discovered this gem shortly before we moved down to Los Angeles. It stands out because of this drink, the Valencia Latte. I'd never had anything like it before—orange blossom and coconut milk infused in an espresso shot? I even got my sister on board, and Voyager became our sister hangout spot. (They have great pastries, too! And now they have lines out their door.) After the move, I missed their Valencia latte (and my sister) so much I tinkered in my kitchen lab until I came up with a version that tastes like home.

You can use any orange for this, but Valencia oranges have zest that's easy to shave with a Y-shaped peeler. Also, don't forget to shake the can of coconut milk before you open it!

If it's your first time making Vietnamese coffee, see Finding and Brewing Vietnamese Coffee (page 24).

1 Put the orange zest in a large mug or pint-size glass. Fit a phin (Vietnamese coffee filter) over the mug, fill the filter with the ground coffee, and press the grounds down with the tamping attachment.

2 Leaving the tamp in place, add boiling water to the top of the filter cup, cover, and let drip until no water remains in the filter.

3 When the coffee has finished, remove the filter, stir in the sugar and vanilla, then add the steamed milks to the top of the mug. Drink immediately, with the orange zest right in the mug.

TAKE IT FROM ME Steaming Milk

Warm milk is essential for the perfect latte—and it's so easy to do. You just warm up milk in the microwave for 1 to 2 minutes, until steaming hot, or warm it up in a saucepan. But when milk is steamed or frothed—using the steaming wand on an espresso maker or a frothing wand made just for the job—you get tiny bubbles that give it a lovely, luxurious mouthfeel and a little foam you can use to decorate the top of your drink. It's worth the extra step. But you don't necessarily need the extra gadgets. There are other ways to make perfect foamed milk, too!

SHAKE IT UP: Fill a 16-ounce mason jar about one-quarter of the way with cold milk, close the lid, then shake for 30 seconds. Warm it up in the microwave for a minute, then add to your coffee.

PRESS IT: Fill a French-press coffeemaker about one-quarter of the way with warm milk. Pump the plunger up and down gently for about 1 minute, or until there are plenty of tiny bubbles and the milk looks foamy. It's ready!

BLEND IT: Fill a 32-ounce mason jar about halfway with hot milk, then blend with an immersion blender for about 20 seconds. Ta da!

COLD BUSTER TEA

MAKES 8 to 10 drinks   **TIME** 10 minutes

1 (2-inch) piece fresh ginger (see Note), peeled

1 cup raw honey

1 tablespoon ground turmeric

2 lemons, halved lengthwise, thinly sliced, and seeded

1 orange, halved lengthwise, thinly sliced, and seeded

Hot water

When you're not feeling your best, this tea works wonders. It's inspired by the traditional Korean citron tea, which is a honey and yuzu citrus mixture. While technically not a "tea," this cold buster offers all the soothing goodness of a hot tea to pacify a sore throat when you're sick (and just the right answer if you're looking for a more "natural" solution).

I added turmeric here for its anti-inflammatory properties, and I also used fresh ginger because it's great for soothing coughs. I recommend buying pregrated ginger as an easy shortcut.

1 With a mortar and pestle, grind the ginger into a paste. In a large bowl, mix together the ginger, honey, and turmeric, then stir in the lemons and orange. Mix well.

2 For each serving, put about 2 heaping tablespoons of the mixture into a mug (citrus and all), fill with hot water, and stir to blend.

3 Transfer any leftover citrus mixture to an airtight container and refrigerate up to 1 month. You can use it straight from the fridge when you're ready for more.

Note If you're in a hurry, you can use 2 tablespoons store-bought minced ginger or ginger paste, from a tube or jar.

TAKE IT FROM ME
Finding and Brewing Vietnamese Coffee

Authentic Vietnamese coffee has a very distinctive taste—strong and slightly bitter. Sweetened condensed milk is typically paired with the coffee to create a perfectly balanced bittersweet flavor. Look for a ground coffee variety by Trung Nguyên or Café du Monde, available in many Asian grocery stores. If you can't find those, substitute strong French roast coffee beans in a coarse grind.

To brew Vietnamese coffee, you must get a Vietnamese phin—a small cylindrical metal coffee filter.

1. Start by placing the filter on top of a mug or glass.
2. Add the ground coffee into the filter and press it down with the removable tamp (if you're using a screw-on type, twist just until there's a slight resistance). Add 1 tablespoon of boiling water to let the coffee grounds bloom, about a minute.
3. Continue to pour boiling water into the filter about three-quarters of the way up and let it drip.
4. Place the lid cover on the filter and let the coffee slowly drip for 3 to 5 minutes.
5. Flip the lid cover and use it as a trivet for the filter. Remove the filter from the mug and enjoy the coffee black or with your favorite milk pairing.

VIETNAMESE EGG COFFEE

MAKES one 8-ounce coffee   TIME 10 minutes

3 tablespoons ground Vietnamese coffee (or 2 shots espresso)

Boiling water

2 large fresh, organic egg yolks

1 tablespoon sweetened condensed milk

½ teaspoon vanilla extract

Unsweetened cocoa powder, for dusting

My parents would often take the family out to Pho 54 to eat pho in San Jose when we were younger. Before the soupy noodles arrived at our table, we always had a moment to watch the other diners. As my parents talked, my older sister, Tram, and I would scout for the people ordering something a little different: Vietnamese egg coffee. It's similar to regular Vietnamese coffee, which has a layer of sweetened condensed milk at the bottom, but instead it's topped with a mixture of whipped egg yolks and sweetened condensed milk, which winds up tasting almost like a meringue on top. We thought it strange at the time, but when I think of it now, I can only fondly describe it as something closer to tiramisu in a cup. The rich, soft topping creates a fascinating coffee that triggers my nostalgia for our family's weekend pho trips.

If it's your first time making Vietnamese coffee, see Finding and Brewing Vietnamese Coffee (opposite).

1 Make two shots of espresso or follow the instructions on page 24 to make the coffee.

2 Meanwhile, in a small bowl, with a hand mixer, whip the egg yolks on medium speed until frothy and pale yellow, about 30 seconds. (You can also whisk by hand for 2 to 3 minutes until the eggs are a shade lighter in color than when you started.) Add the condensed milk and vanilla and mix again just until combined.

3 When the coffee has finished, remove the filter, gently pour the egg mixture over the coffee (it will float on top), and dust with cocoa powder. Drink immediately.

TIPS FOR BUZY LIVES
A Note on Sweetened Condensed Milk

Sweetened condensed milk is a staple in Vietnamese coffee culture. Make sure to purchase sweetened condensed milk, not evaporated milk. After you open the can, transfer the contents to a glass jar, seal it, and then keep it in the fridge, where it will last for 2 weeks!

SUPER CHILL COLD BREW

MAKES 3 cups cold brew
TIME 5 minutes, plus at least 6 hours brewing time

3 cups filtered water,
plus more as needed

⅔ cup coarsely ground
coffee beans

We find making cold brews super convenient (and less diluted than regular iced coffees) because they can be made ahead and kept in the fridge for several days. They also pack more caffeine per sip, which is a lucky bonus when you're tired and need that extra boost.

1 Fill a 32-ounce jar with a lid with 3 cups filtered water. Add the ground coffee, stir to blend (make sure all the grounds are wet), then add water to the top of the jar.

2 Close the jar, refrigerate, and let brew for 6 hours or overnight.

3 When ready to serve, strain the coffee through a nut milk bag or a sieve lined with cheesecloth. (If you have a cone-shaped fine-mesh strainer, that works great also.) Enjoy in a tall glass with ice, or chill and use within 3 days.

VIETNAMESE SHAKERATO

MAKES two 16-ounce drinks **TIME** 5 minutes

3 tablespoons ground
Vietnamese coffee
(or 2 shots espresso)

½ cup boiling water

2 tablespoons sweetened
condensed milk

1 cup whole milk

Ice

The word "shakerato" perfectly describes the Italian shaken (not stirred) espresso shot with ice. This recipe mixes that with a traditional Vietnamese *café sua da* to yield a frothy, refreshingly cold, sweet iced latte. Keep in mind that the condensed milk (see A Note on Sweetened Condensed Milk, page 25) helps increase the volume of the velvety foam, so use caution when adding more sweetener, if that's your preference. You can "shakerato" in a cocktail shaker, but a 32-ounce mason jar with a lid also works fine.

If it's your first time making Vietnamese coffee, see Finding and Brewing Vietnamese Coffee (page 24).

1 Make two shots of espresso or follow the instructions on page 24 to make the coffee.

2 Fill a 20-ounce cocktail shaker with the coffee (or espresso shots), condensed milk, and milk. Add ice until the liquid almost reaches the top of the shaker cup, then shake vigorously for 20 to 30 seconds to incorporate the condensed milk. Strain into two 16-ounce glasses filled with ice. Top with foam from the shaker and enjoy!

SWEET LAVENDER LATTE

MAKES one 16-ounce latte or two 8-ounce lattes **TIME** 5 minutes

3 tablespoons ground
Vietnamese coffee
(or 2 shots espresso)

½ cup boiling water

1 to 2 tablespoons Lavender-
Honey Syrup (recipe follows),
to taste

½ teaspoon vanilla extract

1 cup milk of your choice,
steamed (see Steaming Milk,
page 21)

Ground cinnamon, for dusting

After moving to LA, one of our favorite ways to get acquainted with the city was by exploring all the different neighborhood coffee shops. One drink that I kept seeing on menus was a lavender latte. Of course I had to try it and fell in love. Here is my take, with a delicate balance of floral notes from the lavender and honey paired with a powerful and bold java.

If it's your first time making Vietnamese coffee, see Finding and Brewing Vietnamese Coffee (page 24).

1 Fit a phin (Vietnamese coffee filter) over a 16-ounce mug. Fill the filter with the ground coffee and press the grounds down with the tamping attachment. Leaving the tamp in place, add boiling water to the top of the filter cup, cover, and let drip until no water remains in the filter.

2 When the coffee has finished, remove the filter and stir in the lavender syrup and vanilla, then add steamed milk to the top of the mug. Dust with cinnamon and enjoy!

LAVENDER-HONEY SYRUP

MAKES about 1 cup **TIME** 20 minutes

½ cup dried culinary lavender

½ cup honey

Look for dried lavender in the bulk spice section of a large grocery store, sometimes labeled "culinary lavender." You could also get creative with other flavored syrups and substitute the scraped seeds and pod of half a vanilla bean or the zest of an orange for the lavender.

In a small saucepan, bring 1 cup water to a rolling boil. Remove from the heat, stir in the lavender and honey, and let steep for 15 minutes. Strain through a fine-mesh sieve (or a regular sieve lined with a double layer of cheesecloth), pressing on the solids to extract all the liquid, and transfer to an airtight container. Tightly sealed, the syrup will last up to 1 month in the refrigerator.

Note The lavender syrup is also amazing on its own, simply add to a mug of hot water with a squeeze of lemon.

VANILLA-LAVENDER STEAMED MILK

MAKES one 12-ounce drink   **TIME** 5 minutes

1½ cups whole milk or any milk substitute

1 tablespoon Lavender-Honey Syrup (page 28), or to taste

½ teaspoon vanilla extract

I had a really hard time sleeping during my first pregnancy. I'd be exhausted during the day and wide awake come bedtime. The lavender scent was one miracle therapy that helped me relax, and drinking an infused steamed milk before bed finally got me back into a right-side-up routine.

In a medium saucepan, heat the milk until steaming, but not simmering. Pour the milk into a mug. Stir in the syrup and vanilla. Enjoy immediately!

MATCHA THREE WAYS

Matcha was somewhat of a mystery ingredient to me until maybe ten years ago. When I started my YouTube channel, it wasn't a widely available ingredient and I didn't have much experience with it. This bright green matcha tea powder has been touted for its super antioxidant powers and health benefits, so everyone began making everything with matcha. Of course I jumped on the bandwagon and fell in love with it. Matcha has this earthy, almost bitter, but nutty flavor that can transform any drink or dessert. I use it in various ways in this book, but here I highlight how versatile it can be in a drink, in everything from a warming hot latte to a refreshing cooler. Try them all for yourself and I know you'll fall in love with matcha, too.

MATCHA AND CONDENSED MILK LATTE
MAKES one 16-ounce latte or two 8-ounce lattes **TIME** 10 minutes

2 teaspoons matcha powder

¼ cup hot water

1 to 2 tablespoons sweetened condensed milk, to taste

1½ cups almond milk (or any other milk), steamed (see Steaming Milk, page 21)

Elevate a traditional matcha latte by adding creamy condensed milk. The sweetness enhances the flavor of the tea.

1 In a 16-ounce mug or two smaller mugs, stir together the matcha powder and hot water, then whisk vigorously until there are no lumps.

2 Stir in the condensed milk, mixing to blend, then fill the rest of the mug(s) with steamed almond milk.

MATCHA AND COCONUT COOLER
MAKES two 16-ounce drinks **TIME** 15 minutes

2 teaspoons matcha powder

1 cup hot water

Ice

2 cups coconut water

This is a refreshing and thirst-quenching drink that also provides just the right kick of caffeine for that afternoon slump.

1 In a bowl, stir together the matcha powder and hot water. With a whisk, stir vigorously until there are no lumps. Let cool completely.

2 Fill two 16-ounce glasses with ice, then add coconut water to come about halfway up the glasses (about 1 cup each). Top with the cooled matcha, stir to combine, and enjoy.

(recipe continues)

MATCHA WHITE HOT CHOCOLATE

MAKES two 12-ounce drinks **TIME** 5 minutes

4 (1¼-inch) cubes white chocolate matcha ganache (from Matcha Chocolate Lava Cakes, page 220)

2 cups whole, soy, or oat milk, steamed (see Steaming Milk, page 21)

Made with the same silky ganache I use in my Matcha Chocolate Lava Cakes (page 220), this is an amazing and cozy treat.

In each of two 12-ounce mugs, stir together 2 of the ganache cubes and about ½ cup of the milk until blended. Divide the remaining milk between the two mugs and serve hot!

TAKE IT FROM ME Making Matcha Tea

Matcha is a whole-leaf Japanese green tea that's been ground into a powder. It has a complex, slightly bitter flavor and has become widely available recently. It tastes best whisked with water at 175°F—which is less than boiling. There are special matcha whisks designed with fine spokes to help separate the tea granules, but a regular whisk also works—just don't forget to whisk well, otherwise your drink can be lumpy.

TIPS FOR BUZY LIVES Mix Up Your Milk!

All these matcha drinks are great with any milk—so use what you have on hand, or experiment with almond, rice, or coconut milk!

ROSE MILK TEA

MAKES two 16-ounce drinks   **TIME** 20 minutes

1 Lapsang souchong tea bag (or any strong black tea)

1 cup boiling water

1 to 2 tablespoons honey, to taste

BOBA

½ cup uncooked black boba pearls

1 tablespoon dark brown sugar

Ice

1 teaspoon rose water

About 1 cup whole milk, or to taste

At the celebrity- and blogger-friendly Alfred Tea Room in West Hollywood, the Rosy Black drink stands out with its duet of floral tones and deep black-tea spice. I make it my own with Lapsang souchong, a smoky Chinese tea variety, and rose water for a soft, perfumed refreshment. (Lapsang souchong is available online, but if you can't find any, substitute with Assam or any strong black tea.) I also enjoy adding slightly sweetened black boba pearls for a little extra texture. You can find boba pearls at any Asian market.

1 In a large measuring cup, combine the tea bag, boiling water, and honey and let steep for 3 to 5 minutes. Remove the tea bag and set aside to cool.

2 **MEANWHILE, MAKE THE BOBA:** In a medium saucepan, bring 5 cups water to a boil. Stir in the boba and simmer over medium-high heat until the boba come to the surface. Cook for 3 minutes, stirring occasionally, then remove from the heat, cover, and let sit for 2 minutes. Drain the boba, then run under water for 30 seconds, transfer to a small bowl, and gently stir in the brown sugar until it dissolves.

3 Divide the boba between two 16-ounce glasses, then fill them with ice. Divide the black tea and rose water between the glasses, then top off with milk and stir to blend. Enjoy with a boba straw.

OVERNIGHT THAI MILK TEA

MAKES four 16-ounce drinks
TIME 10 minutes, plus steeping and chilling time

6 tea bags of strong black tea, such as Assam, Darjeeling, or Ceylon

⅓ cup sugar

3 whole cloves

2 star anise

2 cinnamon sticks

2 green cardamom pods

About 4 cups boiling water

Ice

About 1 cup half-and-half or milk of your choice, to taste

Whenever I walk into a Thai restaurant, I immediately think of my favorite Thai meal combo: pad Thai with a creamy Thai iced tea. That glowing, bright orange elixir is completely hypnotic and a treat every time. When I create Thai tea at home, I do my best to leave out the artificial food coloring and flavor additives that some places use. Steeping black tea with cloves, star anise, cinnamon, and cardamom produces a softer amber color while also generating all the natural, complex flavors that make this drink unique. Almond or coconut milk works as a dairy-free substitute for the half-and-half.

1 In a 32-ounce jar or pitcher, combine the tea bags, sugar, cloves, star anise, cinnamon sticks, and cardamom pods. Add boiling water to the top of the jar and let steep for 2 hours.

2 Remove the tea bags and the spices, give the mixture a quick stir, and let cool to room temperature. Cover and refrigerate overnight.

3 Fill four 16-ounce glasses with ice, divide the spiced tea among the ice-filled glasses, and top with half-and-half. Stir and enjoy!

TURN UP THE BEET DRINK

MAKES two 16-ounce drinks   **TIME** 10 minutes

½ cup fresh or frozen raspberries

½ cup (¾-inch) chunks cooked beets (fresh or frozen)

3 large fresh or frozen strawberries, chopped

¼ cup pomegranate seeds

1 teaspoon vanilla extract

½ teaspoon ground cinnamon

1 to 2 tablespoons maple syrup, to taste

About 2 cups almond milk

Ice

I love a drink that's vibrant, delectable, *and* good for you. This fuchsia-swirled almond milk smoothie is a showstopping breakfast sidekick or coffee alternative on the go. Look for steamed and sliced beets in the refrigerated produce section (or frozen ones if you can't find them) at your local supermarket.

1 In a blender, whirl together the raspberries, beets, strawberries, pomegranate seeds, vanilla, cinnamon, maple syrup, and 1 cup of the almond milk until super smooth (see Note).

2 Fill two 16-ounce glasses with ice and divide the smoothie between the two. Add almond milk to the top of each glass. Mix well and serve!

Note If using frozen berries, you may need to add more of the milk during the blending process to achieve a super-smooth texture.

BREAKFAST
the MVP of meals

I love sleep. It's one of my *most* favorite things to do. That's why I often consider skipping breakfast just to steal a few more minutes. But since getting married and especially since becoming a mom, I've learned to embrace the first meal of the day and now have a few scrumptious morning go-tos. This chapter is all about convenient breakfasts for those always on the run—and then some heartier, weekend-inspired brunch ideas perfect for sharing with family and friends when you have a bit more time to linger over the breakfast table.

MUSHROOM AND KALE SAVORY OATMEAL

SERVES 4   TIME 15 minutes

2 cups rolled oats

4¼ cups water, vegetable broth, or chicken broth

1 teaspoon kosher salt, plus more to taste

2 tablespoons extra-virgin olive oil

1 portobello mushroom, sliced

4 cups kale, stems discarded, chopped

2 tablespoons soy sauce

4 soft-boiled eggs (see Foolproof Soft-Boiled Eggs, below)

Freshly ground black pepper to taste

Kimchi (optional), for serving

I like to start my day with some greens when I can. It makes me feel energized and a bit healthier, so I've been putting some sautéed kale and mushrooms into this savory oatmeal, and it leaves me pretty satisfied. This recipe is packed with umami, and if you want additional texture and punch, I recommend adding some kimchi on top.

1 In a medium saucepan, combine the oats, water, and kosher salt. Cook over medium heat, stirring once or twice, until the water is fully absorbed, about 10 minutes. Cover and set aside.

2 Meanwhile, heat a large skillet over medium heat. Add the olive oil, then the mushroom, and cook, stirring occasionally, until softened, 3 to 5 minutes. Add the kale, soy sauce, and 2 tablespoons water and continue cooking and stirring until the kale is wilted, about 3 more minutes. Set aside.

3 Divide the oatmeal among four bowls, top with the vegetables, and drizzle any sauce left at the bottom of the skillet on top. Add a soft-boiled egg to each bowl, season to taste with salt and pepper, and serve immediately, with kimchi, if desired.

TAKE IT FROM ME Foolproof Soft-Boiled Eggs

I love steaming my eggs because it makes them easier to peel. And it's simple! Pour about 1 inch of water into a large saucepan or pot with a tight-fitting lid and set a steamer basket in the bottom. Bring the water to a simmer. Add as many large eggs as you want, cover tightly, and steam 6 to 7 minutes for a soft-boiled egg or 10 minutes for an egg that's firm almost all the way through (hard-cooked, but still a bit moist in the center). Transfer the eggs to a bowl of ice water to make them easier to peel; you can peel them as soon as it's comfortable to touch them. You can also refrigerate the eggs, unpeeled, for up to 3 days before using.

OVERNIGHT OATS FOUR WAYS

Overnight oats are an ideal breakfast because they're make-ahead and super satisfying. They're more filling than regular oatmeal because of all the protein from the Greek yogurt—and the yogurt gives it a creaminess that makes it more like pudding (and never soggy). I love how customizable they can be as well: Oatmeal can support almost any flavor combination! Experiment with different fruits, or even try almond, rice, or coconut milk instead of what I use below.

I divide these recipes between two 7 or 8 ounce jars, leaving a bit of room at the top for a few scoops of yummy toppings. If you want a heartier breakfast, you could make it just one serving.

CHERRY-ALMOND OVERNIGHT OATS

SERVES 2 **TIME** 15 minutes, plus refrigeration time

1 cup fresh pitted or frozen cherries

1 tablespoon maple syrup or honey

½ cup plain Greek yogurt

½ cup whole milk

½ teaspoon vanilla extract

¼ teaspoon almond extract

½ cup rolled oats

1 tablespoon sliced almonds (optional)

This is a healthier twist on French clafoutis, the dessert traditionally made with cherries and sometimes almond extract. I like using frozen dark cherries, because they're available all year long, but using fresh cherries would also work if you're making these when cherries are in season.

1 In a medium saucepan, combine ½ cup of the cherries, 2 tablespoons water, and the maple syrup and cook over medium heat, stirring occasionally, until the cherries have released their juices and softened, about 7 minutes. Give the cherries a gentle mash with a large fork or spoon and set aside to cool for 10 minutes.

2 In a bowl, stir together the yogurt, milk, vanilla, and almond extract. Add the cooled cherry compote and the oats and stir again.

3 Pour the mixture into two 8-ounce jars or a large container and refrigerate for 4 hours or overnight. (The oats keep well for up to 3 days.)

4 To serve, top with the remaining cherries and sliced almonds (if using).

CREAMY VANILLA-ORANGE OVERNIGHT OATS

SERVES 2 **TIME** 5 minutes, plus refrigeration time

½ cup plain Greek yogurt

¼ cup whole milk

1 teaspoon grated orange zest

¼ cup orange juice

½ teaspoon vanilla extract

½ cup rolled oats

Segments from 1 small navel orange, chopped

Who doesn't love a throwback to a creamy orange Popsicle? It's a timeless flavor, and for a good reason—it's delicious.

1 In a bowl, stir together the yogurt, milk, orange zest and juice, and vanilla. Add the oats and mix again.

2 Pour the mixture into two 8-ounce jars or a large container and

refrigerate for 4 hours or overnight. (The oats keep well for up to 3 days.)

3 To serve, top with chopped orange segments.

(recipe continues)

BLACKBERRY-GINGER OVERNIGHT OATS

SERVES 2   **TIME** 5 minutes, plus refrigeration time

1 cup blackberries

½ cup plain Greek yogurt

½ cup whole milk

1 tablespoon maple syrup
or honey

½ teaspoon grated peeled
fresh ginger

½ teaspoon vanilla extract

½ cup rolled oats

I love the fresh, tangy flavor of berries and ginger together. Be sure
to mash the blackberries well, so they are evenly distributed among
the oats.

1 In a bowl, mash half the
blackberries well with a fork, then
add the yogurt, milk, maple syrup,
ginger, and vanilla and stir together.
Add the oats and mix again.

2 Pour the mixture into two
8-ounce jars or a large container and
refrigerate for 4 hours or overnight.
(The oats keep well for up to 3 days.)

3 To serve, top with the remaining
blackberries.

BANANA CREAM PIE OVERNIGHT OATS

SERVES 2   **TIME** 5 minutes, plus refrigeration time

1 very ripe banana

1 tablespoon caramel sauce
(from a jar)

1 tablespoon chia seeds

½ cup plain Greek yogurt

½ cup whole milk

½ teaspoon vanilla extract

½ cup rolled oats

1 teaspoon shaved high-quality
chocolate, for topping

At Tartine, in San Francisco, there's a tart that might be the world's
best version of banana cream pie. It has a thin layer of chocolate
on the bottom, followed by a layer of caramel, then bananas, pastry
cream, a cloud of whipped cream, and chocolate shavings on top.
Here's a breakfast version, but I wouldn't rule out eating it for dessert.

1 In a bowl, mash together the
banana, caramel sauce, and chia
seeds with a fork, then stir in the
yogurt, milk, and vanilla. Mix well.
Add the oats and mix again.

2 Pour the mixture into two
8-ounce jars or a large container and
refrigerate for 4 hours or overnight.
(The oats keep well for up to 3 days.)

3 To serve, sprinkle half the shaved
chocolate on top of each and enjoy.

FARMERS' MARKET AVOCADO TOAST

MAKES 1 toast   **TIME** 10 minutes

1 thick slice hearty artisanal bread (such as a country loaf or sourdough)

1 garlic clove, peeled

½ medium avocado

½ teaspoon lemon juice

Kosher salt and freshly ground black pepper

2 tablespoons microgreens (such as radish, kale, or sunflower)

1 small radish, thinly sliced

2 teaspoons pumpkin seeds, toasted (see Note)

1 tablespoon crumbled queso fresco or other crumbly cheese (such as feta or goat cheese)

California farmers' markets offer a diverse selection of locally grown, seasonal produce that always tastes like peak freshness. California Hass avocados have the creamiest mouthfeel to create those ubiquitous, worth-the-$10, Instagram-friendly avocado toasts. I'll admit that I'm a sucker for these delights, but I actually do make them for myself, fairly often, usually for breakfast or a light lunch. While I'm at the market I'll also pick up a few other ingredients like radishes, microgreens, and pumpkin seeds, which all make for crunchy, healthy toppings. I cut pretty thick slices of bread, so sometimes I cut and eat the toast with a fork and knife.

1 Toast the bread until lightly golden brown. Take the garlic clove and rub it all over the toast.

2 In a bowl, mash the avocado with the lemon juice and salt and pepper to taste. Spread the mashed avocado onto the toast. Top with the greens and sliced radish, sprinkle with the pumpkin seeds and queso fresco, and serve.

Note Heat a skillet (cast-iron or nonstick both work) over medium-low heat and add the pumpkin seeds. Let them toast for about 5 minutes, shaking the pan occasionally to avoid burning. Remove from the heat and let the seeds continue toasting in the hot pan for another 5 minutes, shaking occasionally. Let cool.

MANGO-TURMERIC SMOOTHIE BOWLS

MAKES 2 smoothie bowls   **TIME** 10 minutes

2 cups frozen mango chunks

2 very ripe bananas

1 cup plain Greek yogurt

½ cup whole milk of your choice

2 teaspoons vanilla extract

1 teaspoon ground turmeric

Dash of ground cinnamon

About ½ cup sliced dragon fruit or berries (such as strawberries or raspberries)

About ½ cup diced papaya

1 tablespoon chia seeds

2 tablespoons unsweetened coconut flakes

If you're ever on the North Shore of Oahu, Hawaii, be sure to make a stop at the Sunrise Shack in Hale'iwa. Their smoothie bowls are legendary. I got one topped with some beautiful Hawaiian papaya. I loved how the bowls came icy-cold with some healthy add-ins. After getting back to LA, I created this easy mango smoothie bowl, which is built on frozen mango with a mixture of colorful tropical ingredients. I recommend chopped dates, sliced almonds, toasted pistachios, or flaxseeds as other topping ideas.

In a blender, combine the mango, 1 of the bananas, yogurt, milk, vanilla, turmeric, and cinnamon. Blend on high speed until you get a thick puree. (If the blender gets stuck, add 2 more tablespoons milk to get it moving.) Slice the remaining banana. Pour the smoothie into a bowl and top with the sliced banana, dragon fruit, papaya, chia seeds, and coconut flakes. Enjoy!

APRICOT-WALNUT-CARDAMOM GRANOLA YOGURT CUPS

MAKES about 8 cups   **TIME** 45 minutes, plus cooling time

FOR THE GRANOLA

4 cups rolled oats

1 cup walnut halves or pieces

½ cup pumpkin seeds

½ cup white sesame seeds

2 teaspoons ground cardamom

1 teaspoon ground cinnamon

1 teaspoon ground ginger

1 teaspoon kosher salt

½ cup melted coconut oil or avocado oil

½ cup honey or maple syrup

2 tablespoons dark brown sugar

1 teaspoon vanilla extract

1½ cups dried apricots, chopped

FOR THE CUPS

Vanilla or plain Greek yogurt

Honey

Granola is super convenient to have on hand. It goes well with milk for a quick cereal-like snack or, better yet, on top of a yogurt cup like we have here. I like the walnuts in this recipe because they pair well with apricots, but feel free to use any type of nut you prefer.

1 Preheat the oven to 325°F. Line a rimmed baking sheet with parchment paper.

2 In a large bowl, stir together the oats, walnuts, pumpkin seeds, sesame seeds, cardamom, cinnamon, ginger, and salt.

3 In a small bowl, whisk together the melted coconut oil, honey, brown sugar, and vanilla. Pour the liquids over the oat mixture. Mix thoroughly, so that the oats are evenly coated.

4 Transfer the granola to the prepared baking sheet and pat into a thin, even layer. Bake for 15 minutes. Remove from the oven, give the mixture a thorough mix with a spoon or spatula, then pat it back down. (This will help it crisp.)

Return the pan to the oven and bake for another 15 to 20 minutes, until the granola is evenly baked and golden brown, rotating the pan once halfway during this second baking. (If the oats on the edges of the pan start to brown faster than the rest of the granola, give it another stir.)

5 Remove the granola from the oven and let cool completely (about 45 minutes). Stir in the chopped apricots. Store the granola in an airtight container at room temperature for up to 1 week, or freeze up to 1 month.

6 To build a yogurt cup, fill a glass jar or cup about halfway with yogurt. Top with a scoop of granola, drizzle with honey, and enjoy! (You can also just eat the granola with milk.)

CHEESY EVERYTHING BAGEL BISCUITS

MAKES 6 biscuits **TIME** 45 minutes

3 large eggs

⅓ cup whole milk

2 cups all-purpose flour, plus more for dusting

1 tablespoon plus 1 teaspoon everything bagel seasoning

2 teaspoons mustard powder (such as Colman's)

1 tablespoon baking powder

1 teaspoon kosher salt

¼ teaspoon cayenne pepper (optional)

6 tablespoons (¾ stick) cold unsalted butter, grated with a cheese grater

1 cup grated sharp cheddar cheese

Everything bagels are one of my favorite breakfast treats. Too bad they're very time consuming to make at home. So I came up with these cheesy everything bagel biscuits. All the right spices are here, like poppy seeds, dried onion flakes, garlic, and sesame seeds—but instead of a round chewy bread, they're infused into flaky, cheesy, buttery biscuits. They can be served plain or cut open, spread with cream cheese, and topped with bacon or a fried egg for a mouthwatering breakfast sandwich.

1 Preheat the oven to 375°F. Lightly grease a baking sheet or line it with parchment paper.

2 In a small bowl, mix together 2 of the eggs and the milk until blended.

3 In a large bowl, whisk together the flour, 1 tablespoon of the bagel seasoning, the mustard powder, baking powder, salt, and cayenne (if using). Work in the butter with your fingers to make an unevenly crumbly mixture, then stir in the cheddar. Add the milk and egg mixture to the dry ingredients, stirring with a wooden spoon just until everything is evenly moistened; the dough will be sticky.

4 Liberally flour your hands and a clean work surface. Turn the dough onto the counter, then pat it into a 12 × 2-inch rectangle. Cut the

dough into six 2-inch circles using a round biscuit cutter or a glass. Brush excess flour off the biscuits, then transfer them to the prepared baking sheet, leaving at least 1 inch between them. At this point, you can cover the biscuits with plastic wrap and refrigerate for at least 1 hour and up to 24 hours before baking.

5 When ready to bake, in a small bowl, whisk the remaining egg with 2 teaspoons water until blended. Brush the egg mixture onto each biscuit and sprinkle them with the remaining 1 teaspoon bagel seasoning.

6 Bake the biscuits for 20 to 23 minutes, until they're nicely browned. Cool for 5 minutes, then enjoy warm.

TAKE IT FROM ME Keep It Cold

For the fluffiest biscuits, make sure the butter is extra cold before baking. The cold butter creates steam as it melts, leaving pockets of air and layers as the biscuit bakes.

CHIA PUDDING FOUR WAYS

Chia puddings are another fantastic make-ahead, grab 'n' go breakfast. They're nutritious and filling and can be flavored almost any way you'd like. Whether you're feeling like a cinnamon-forward horchata in the afternoon or a midmorning jolt of cold brew, these puddings are infinitely customizable.

When the chia seeds begin to soak up liquid, they can clump together a bit. To avoid this, simply stir the puddings (or if they're in a jar, shake them) about 15 minutes after you make them. For two snacks, you can divide the stirred mixture for each recipe between two jars before letting it soak overnight.

RASPBERRY LEMONADE CHIA PUDDING
MAKES 2 puddings **TIME** 10 minutes, plus refrigeration time

¼ cup fresh raspberries, plus a handful for serving

1 tablespoon maple syrup

1 teaspoon grated lemon zest

1 tablespoon lemon juice

1 teaspoon vanilla extract

1 cup coconut milk beverage (from a carton) or almond milk (see Note, page 56)

¼ cup chia seeds

1 In a bowl, mash the raspberries with a fork or spoon, then mix with the maple syrup, lemon zest, lemon juice, and vanilla. Add the milk and stir to blend. Stir in the chia seeds and refrigerate for 4 hours or overnight. (The puddings keep well, refrigerated, up to 3 days.)

2 To serve, divide the pudding between two bowls (or two small mason jars), top with more raspberries, and enjoy.

HORCHATA CHIA PUDDING
MAKES 2 puddings **TIME** 10 minutes, plus refrigeration time

2 tablespoons plain yogurt or coconut milk yogurt

1 tablespoon maple syrup

1 teaspoon vanilla extract

½ teaspoon ground cinnamon

Pinch of kosher salt

1 cup rice milk beverage (from a carton; see Note, page 56)

¼ cup chia seeds

Sliced strawberries and blueberries, for serving

1 In a bowl, stir together the yogurt, maple syrup, vanilla, cinnamon, and salt. Add the rice milk and stir to blend. Stir in the chia seeds and refrigerate for at least 4 hours or overnight. (The puddings keep well, refrigerated, up to 3 days.)

2 To serve, divide the pudding between two bowls (or two small mason jars), top with the berries, and enjoy.

(recipe continues)

COLD BREW CHIA PUDDING

MAKES 2 puddings **TIME** 10 minutes, plus refrigeration time

1 tablespoon maple syrup

1 teaspoon vanilla extract

¼ teaspoon unsweetened cocoa powder

½ cup cold brew coffee, store-bought or homemade (page 26)

½ cup coconut milk beverage (from a carton) or almond milk (see Note)

¼ cup chia seeds

Sliced strawberries and chocolate shavings, for serving

1 In a bowl, stir together the maple syrup, vanilla, and cocoa powder. Add the coffee and milk and stir to blend. Stir in the chia seeds and refrigerate for at least 4 hours or overnight. (The puddings keep well, refrigerated, up to 3 days.)

2 To serve, divide the pudding between two bowls (or two small mason jars), top with strawberries and chocolate shavings, and enjoy.

KEY LIME PIE CHIA PUDDING

MAKES 2 puddings **TIME** 10 minutes, plus refrigeration time

2 tablespoons plain yogurt or coconut milk yogurt

1 tablespoon maple syrup

1 teaspoon vanilla extract

1 teaspoon grated lime zest, plus more for serving

1 to 2 tablespoons lime juice (depending on how sour you'd like it)

1 cup coconut milk beverage (from a carton; see Note)

¼ cup chia seeds

Greek yogurt, for serving

Crumbled graham cracker, for serving

1 In a bowl, stir together the yogurt, maple syrup, vanilla, lime zest, and lime juice. Add the coconut milk beverage and stir to blend. Stir in the chia seeds and refrigerate for at least 4 hours or overnight. (The puddings keep well, refrigerated, up to 3 days.)

2 To serve, divide the pudding between two bowls (or two small mason jars), top with a dollop of yogurt, some lime zest, and the graham cracker crumbs, and enjoy.

Note You can use cow's, almond, rice, and coconut milks interchangeably here. I always use unsweetened milks so I can sweeten to taste, but flavored versions also work.

TAKE IT FROM ME You Need a Snack

While chia pudding makes a great breakfast, it also works as a snack. I like to make this quartet of puddings over the weekend whenever I have a few minutes free, so I have a grab-and-go option ready anytime during the week.

KOREAN BEEF HASH

SERVES 2 to 4   TIME 45 minutes (using leftover short ribs)

1½ pounds Yukon Gold potatoes (about 5 medium)

Kosher salt

2 tablespoons extra-virgin olive oil

½ yellow onion, chopped

½ red bell pepper, chopped

2 garlic cloves, finely chopped

1 teaspoon smoked paprika

2 cups shredded braised short rib meat (from Korean Braised Short Ribs, page 165)

2 tablespoons chopped fresh flat-leaf parsley

4 large eggs

Freshly ground black pepper

Sometimes leftovers make the best breakfasts, don't you agree? Whenever I make *galbijjim,* I take whatever spicy shredded meat is left over and add it to this crispy potato hash. It just has the most satisfying flavors of both a classic American breakfast and an indulgent Korean feast.

For this recipe, you'll need to start by making Korean Braised Short Ribs and saving about 2 cups of the delicious braised meat. Serve with kimchi, if you like a little spice.

1 Put the potatoes in a large saucepan and add cold water to cover. Add 1 tablespoon salt and bring to a boil over medium-high heat. Cook until tender, 7 to 9 minutes. Drain and let cool. Once cool enough to handle, cut the potatoes into ¾-inch pieces.

2 Preheat the oven to 425°F.

3 In a large cast-iron skillet, heat the oil over medium-high heat. Once the oil is hot, add the onion and sauté until translucent and fragrant, 3 to 4 minutes. Add the bell pepper, garlic, and smoked paprika and cook for another 3 minutes, stirring frequently. Add the shredded beef and cook until the fat from the beef coats the bottom of the pan. Stir in the potatoes and cook until they begin to soften, about 5 minutes, stirring occasionally. (If the potatoes stick, drizzle 2 tablespoons water over everything and stir.) Stir in the parsley.

4 With a spoon, make four egg-size hollows in between the potatoes and meat and crack an egg into each one. Season with salt and pepper to taste.

5 Transfer the skillet to the oven and bake for 6 to 10 minutes, until the egg whites are mostly firm but the yolks are still slightly runny. (You can bake longer if you prefer a more cooked egg yolk, but remember that the eggs will continue to cook once the dish comes out of the oven.) Serve and enjoy!

EGG AND CHORIZO BREAKFAST BURRITOS

MAKES 4 burritos **TIME** 30 minutes

2 teaspoons extra-virgin olive oil

½ pound bulk chorizo sausage

6 large eggs

Kosher salt and freshly ground black pepper

1 tablespoon unsalted butter (optional)

4 burrito-size flour tortillas (10 or 12 inches)

½ cup shredded cheddar cheese

1 avocado, sliced

4 to 8 tablespoons Quick Chipotle Salsa (recipe follows)

Nate is our resident burrito expert. He has his go-to spots but can usually whip up some good ones at home, too. Early during my second pregnancy I'd become ravenously "hangry," often right before we started filming a cooking tutorial, so he would quickly make me a protein-packed egg and chorizo burrito. Hmm, maybe this recipe should be called the "Hangry Monster Burrito"? We've been in this situation often enough to start freezing them ahead of time, avocados and all! The chipotle salsa comes together surprisingly quick in a blender, but if you're in a rush, store-bought salsa is great, too. I like to add some tangy kimchi to mine (of course).

1 Heat a medium cast-iron skillet over medium heat. Add the olive oil, then crumble the chorizo into the pan. Cook, stirring and breaking up the sausage as it cooks, until it's completely cooked through, 7 to 10 minutes. Remove from the pan and set aside.

2 In a large bowl, whisk the eggs with salt and pepper to taste until evenly yellow. Return the skillet to medium-low heat and add the butter (if your chorizo left plenty of fat in the pan, you may opt to skip the butter). When the butter has melted, tilt the pan to cover the bottom, then add the eggs. Let them set for about a minute, or until they've just cooked across the bottom of the pan, then use a silicone spatula to stir and scrape

the eggs off the bottom, stirring constantly until the eggs are fluffy and mostly set. (You don't want the eggs to be completely cooked, as they'll continue cooking after you remove them from the pan.) Transfer the eggs to a plate.

3 Heat the tortillas, transfer them to plates, then add 2 tablespoons of the shredded cheddar, one-quarter of the scrambled eggs, avocado slices, one-quarter of the cooked chorizo, and 1 to 2 tablespoons of the salsa to each tortilla. Wrap and enjoy hot. (If you need to keep them warm for a few minutes, simply place the burritos seam-side down in a clean nonstick skillet over low heat. This step also makes the outsides a bit crispy, which is just how I like my burritos.)

TAKE IT FROM ME Heating Tortillas

Heat up the tortillas in a stack in the microwave for about 30 seconds just before using them, or, if you have a gas range, simply toast them over a low flame for a few seconds on each side.

(recipe continues)

QUICK CHIPOTLE SALSA

MAKES about 1½ cups **TIME** 10 minutes

2 Roma (plum) tomatoes, cut into chunks

¼ yellow onion, cut into chunks

8 sprigs fresh cilantro

1 garlic clove, peeled

1 whole chipotle pepper in adobo sauce

Juice of ½ lime

The secret to this super-quick salsa is a blender, which allows you to make salsa with not much more than the press of a button. I also add a smoky chipotle pepper to give it a spicy kick. You can find canned chipotle peppers in adobo sauce in the Hispanic sections of any large or well-stocked grocery store.

1 In a blender, combine the tomatoes, onion, cilantro, garlic, chipotle, and lime juice. Blend until the salsa reaches your desired consistency. (I like mine chunky.)

2 Set aside the salsa at room temperature until ready to use, or cover and refrigerate up to 3 days.

GET YOUR GREENS SMOOTHIE

MAKES two 12-ounce smoothies   TIME 10 minutes

1 cup packed spinach
or kale leaves

1 Persian (mini) cucumber,
cut into large chunks

½ avocado

½ green apple, cored and
quartered

½ banana

½ cup chopped fresh pineapple

1 tablespoon chia seeds

1 cup coconut water or water

1 cup ice (4 standard ice cubes)

Smoothies are an easy way to get some healthy veggies and fruits into your day, especially when you can't bring yourself to eat them otherwise. I blend my leafy greens with cooling vegetables and tart fruits to make a refreshing smoothie. Even Erisy loves this recipe! If you like a spicy kick to your smoothie, add ½ teaspoon grated peeled fresh ginger.

In a blender, whirl together the spinach, cucumber, avocado, apple, banana, pineapple, chia, coconut water, and ice until smooth. Pour into two glasses and serve immediately.

CREPES *with* GOAT CHEESE–SCRAMBLED EGGS

SERVES 4 to 6 **TIME** 25 minutes

FOR THE CREPES

¾ cup whole milk

½ cup all-purpose flour

2 large eggs

2 tablespoons unsalted butter, melted

1 teaspoon sugar

½ teaspoon kosher salt

FOR THE EGGS

8 large eggs

1 teaspoon kosher salt

Freshly ground black pepper

2 tablespoons unsalted butter

2 tablespoons chopped fresh chives, dill, or tarragon, plus more for serving

3 tablespoons crumbled goat cheese

If you think you can only enjoy a delicious breakfast crepe at a fancy French café, think again. Crepes are actually not that hard to make! They do take a bit of technique and patience, but once you get the hang of it, they're a breeze. I recommend using a nonstick skillet rather than a traditional steel crepe pan because it releases the crepes better, making them easier to flip.

The crepe batter here is your blank canvas, so feel free to make your crepes sweet with Nutella, strawberries, and whipped cream.

1 **MAKE THE CREPE BATTER:** In a blender, whirl together the milk, flour, eggs, 1 tablespoon of the melted butter, the sugar, and salt until well blended. (You can make the batter ahead of time and store it in the fridge overnight. Stir or shake the batter before using.)

2 Heat an 8- or 10-inch nonstick pan over medium heat. Brush a thin layer of the remaining melted butter across the entire bottom of the pan, then add about ¼ cup of the batter. Swirl to cover the surface of the pan immediately. (Depending on your pan size and swirling technique, you may need more or less batter.) Cook the crepe until the edges start to curl, about 1 minute, then use a thin spatula to gently flip the crepe and cook until the second side has browned, another 30 seconds. Transfer the crepe to a plate and repeat with the remaining batter, brushing the pan again with butter every other crepe or so, and adjusting the temperature as needed to make sure the crepes are browning well (but not burning).

Be sure to give the batter a mix each time before adding more to the pan.

3 **ONCE YOU GET THE CREPES COOKING, START THE EGGS:** (If you're not ready to multitask, wait until you finish all the crepes!) In a large bowl, whisk the eggs with the salt and pepper to taste. Heat a large nonstick skillet over medium-low heat and add the butter. When the butter has melted, tilt the pan to cover the bottom, then add the eggs. Let them set until they've just cooked against the bottom of the pan, about 1 minute, then use a silicone spatula to stir and scrape the eggs off the bottom, stirring constantly until the eggs are fluffy and mostly set. Stir in the chives and the goat cheese, then transfer the eggs to a plate.

4 To serve, spread a crepe out on a plate. Place one-quarter to one-sixth of the eggs in the center of the crepe, then fold the edges up from four sides, so the crepe forms a square. Serve hot, garnished with chives.

VIETNAMESE PAN-FRIED RICE CAKES (BÁNH BỘT CHIÊN)

SERVES 4 to 6 **TIME** 1 hour, plus cooling time

5 tablespoons neutral-tasting oil (such as avocado oil), plus more for the pan

2 cups packed grated peeled daikon radish (about 10 ounces)

2 cups white rice flour

3 tablespoons cornstarch

½ teaspoon kosher salt

½ teaspoon sugar

6 large eggs, lightly whisked to blend

Roughly chopped fresh cilantro, for serving

Soy Dipping Sauce (recipe follows)

These rice flour cakes are a street food favorite in Vietnam. I was first introduced to them when my dad would take the family to Tung Kee Noodle House in Santa Clara. These rice cakes make for an unexpected Western breakfast, especially with my addition of the daikon radish, but I promise you'll be amazed.

It can seem like quite the process, but if you make the rice cake loaf ahead and refrigerate it overnight, all you need to do is cut and pan-fry the cakes in the morning! Fresh and hot is the only way to enjoy these chewy, savory little rice pillows. Serve with Vietnamese coffee for an authentic breakfast!

1 To steam, find a large pot with a lid that fits a 9 × 5-inch loaf pan inside, with the pot lid securely closed. Fill the pot with about 1 inch of water, then insert a steaming rack (if necessary, adjust the water so it comes just up to, but not above, the steaming rack). Bring to a simmer while you work.

2 Grease a 9 × 5-inch loaf pan with oil and set aside.

3 Heat a large nonstick or seasoned cast-iron skillet over medium heat. Add 1 tablespoon of the oil and the grated daikon. Cook and stir until the daikon has softened, about 10 minutes. (Adjust the heat as needed to make sure it doesn't brown.)

4 Meanwhile, in a large bowl, whisk together the rice flour, cornstarch, salt, and sugar. Add 3 cups water and whisk the batter until smooth.

5 Once the daikon is soft, pour the batter into the skillet, stirring

constantly, and continue stirring for a few minutes, until the mixture forms a thick paste. It should have the consistency of thick glue or paint. (The exact timing will depend on how hot your pan is.)

6 Transfer the daikon batter to the prepared loaf pan and place the pan in the steamer. Cover and steam over medium-high heat (or hot enough for the water to remain at a hard simmer) until the flour cake is firm in the center, about 25 minutes, adding boiling water as necessary to keep the water level just under the loaf pan. Remove the pan from the heat and transfer to a rack to let cool completely. (Once the cake is cool, you can cover the cake and refrigerate until ready to serve, up to 3 days, or wrap in plastic and freeze for up to 1 month.)

7 When ready to serve, remove the cake from the pan and cut it into 1-inch-thick pieces. Cut smaller pieces if you prefer. (You may have

(recipe continues)

to pry the cake away from the pan—that's okay!)

8 In a large skillet, heat 2 tablespoons of the oil over medium-high heat. When hot, add half of the rice flour cakes and fry until golden brown on one side, 3 to 4 minutes. Gently flip the cakes, then add half the eggs, pouring them into the pan right over the cakes. (They should be a pretty mixture of white and yellow, not all blended together.) Cover and cook until the eggs are completely cooked, another 3 to 4 minutes.

9 Slide the cakes and eggs onto a serving plate. Garnish with cilantro and serve with the soy dipping sauce. Wipe out the pan. Repeat with the remaining 2 tablespoons oil, cakes, and eggs.

SOY DIPPING SAUCE

MAKES ½ cup   **TIME** 5 minutes

This sauce is perfect for dipping or drizzling on the cakes, or for Kimchi Pancakes (page 194).

½ cup soy sauce

2 teaspoons rice vinegar

2 teaspoons honey

½ teaspoon sriracha

¼ teaspoon sesame oil

In a bowl, whisk together the soy sauce, vinegar, honey, sriracha, and sesame oil until the honey has dissolved.

ORANGE-PISTACHIO FRENCH TOAST

MAKES 8 slices   **TIME** 25 minutes

FOR THE SPICED SYRUP

1 cup maple syrup

½ teaspoon ground cinnamon

¼ teaspoon ground cardamom

1 (2-inch) strip orange zest
(see Note)

FOR THE FRENCH TOAST

3 large eggs

2 tablespoons dark brown sugar

¼ teaspoon ground cinnamon

½ cup whole milk

Grated zest and juice of 1 large
orange (see Note)

Pinch of salt

Unsalted butter, for the pan

8 (1-inch-thick) slices brioche

FOR SERVING

1½ cups raspberries
(about 6 ounces)

¼ cup chopped pistachios

If we're out for brunch and I'm craving something sweet, French toast is the way to go. The crispy bite and fluffy chew, oozing with syrup and usually topped with more goodness, is a moment in heaven. In my own kitchen, I love to experiment with different spices and breads to see how far I can take French toast. I've gotten pretty crazy with toasts before. (Have you seen my "25 Epic Toasts" video?) But this orange-pistachio French toast takes on a more elevated vibe.

You could also use sliced baguette or any thick and hearty bread in place of the brioche.

1 **MAKE THE SYRUP:** In a small saucepan, whisk together the maple syrup, cinnamon, and cardamom. Add the orange zest and bring to a simmer, then cook for 3 minutes. Remove the orange zest and set the syrup aside until ready to serve.

2 **MEANWHILE, MAKE THE FRENCH TOAST:** In a large shallow bowl or baking dish, whisk together the eggs, brown sugar, and cinnamon until thoroughly blended. Add the milk, orange zest, orange juice, and salt and whisk to combine.

3 Heat a large nonstick pan over medium heat. When hot, add about 2 teaspoons butter, moving it around until the pan is coated. As the butter melts, soak 2 slices of the brioche on each side for about 15 seconds in the egg mixture. Transfer the bread to the pan and cook until golden brown on both sides and set in the center, 3 to 4 minutes per side. Repeat with the remaining bread and egg mixture, adding a bit more butter as needed.

4 Serve the French toast drizzled with the syrup and topped with raspberries and pistachios.

Note You only need 1 orange for this recipe—take a strip of zest off first for the syrup, then use the rest of the zest and the juice for the egg mixture.

MATCHA-ALMOND BREAKFAST LOAF

MAKES 1 loaf   **TIME** 1 hour, plus cooling time

Butter and flour, for the pan

FOR THE CRUMBLE TOPPING

1 tablespoon unsalted butter, melted

2 tablespoons all-purpose flour

1 tablespoon granulated sugar

1 tablespoon dark brown sugar

¼ teaspoon kosher salt

Dash of ground cinnamon

¼ cup sliced almonds

FOR THE BREAD

1½ cups all-purpose flour

1 teaspoon baking powder

½ teaspoon kosher salt

1 tablespoon matcha powder

8 tablespoons (1 stick) unsalted butter, melted

¾ cup granulated sugar

2 large eggs

1 teaspoon vanilla extract

½ teaspoon almond extract

¾ cup whole milk, at room temperature

When I worked in corporate finance I'd often come home after work and immediately continue my daily baking challenge. I got really into quick breads (like banana, blueberry-lemon, or pumpkin loaves) and shared so much with my colleagues and friends that I was soon dubbed the "Quick Bread Queen." I mean, what's better than some homemade bread to have on hand for breakfast, right? This matcha-almond loaf, topped with a crunchy brown sugar crumble, is something I like to share with my friends and neighbors.

1 Preheat the oven to 350°F. Grease a 9 × 5-inch loaf pan with butter, dust with flour, and shake out the excess flour.

2 MAKE THE CRUMBLE TOPPING: In a small bowl, combine the melted butter, flour, granulated sugar, dark brown sugar, salt, and cinnamon until evenly moist. Add the almonds, mix again, and set aside.

3 MAKE THE BREAD: In a small bowl, whisk together the flour, baking powder, salt, and matcha powder. Set aside.

4 In a large bowl, whisk together the melted butter and granulated sugar. Add the eggs one at a time, whisking after each addition until the eggs are completely incorporated. Add the vanilla and almond extract and mix again.

5 Add about half the flour mixture to the butter mixture and fold it in until mostly incorporated. Stir in the milk, then add the remaining flour mixture and fold it in until just incorporated. (Make sure not to overmix the batter or it will get tough—it's okay if the batter is still a bit lumpy.) Pour the batter into the prepared baking pan, top with the crumble mixture, and use your fingers to press the crumble gently into the batter.

6 Bake the loaf for 40 to 45 minutes, until puffed and golden on top and a toothpick inserted in the center comes out clean. Let cool for 15 minutes in the pan, then unmold onto a cooling rack to cool completely before serving. Wrap any unsliced bread well and store at room temperature for up to 2 days.

SALADS & SOUPS

a seasonal take

Living in California, I can count on sourcing the freshest seasonal vegetables and herbs for my soups and salads. A colorful, filling salad works year-round, while soup covers those chillier days (yes, even in LA).

SPRING FARRO AND VEGGIE SALAD

SERVES 4 to 6   **TIME** 35 minutes

FOR THE FARRO

2 teaspoons kosher salt

½ cup farro

FOR THE LEMON-DIJON DRESSING

2 tablespoons lemon juice

2 tablespoons extra-virgin olive oil

1 tablespoon Dijon mustard

1 tablespoon honey

1 teaspoon kosher salt

½ teaspoon freshly ground black pepper

FOR THE SALAD

2 teaspoons kosher salt

6 ounces sugar snap peas, halved on the diagonal (about 2 cups)

1 bunch asparagus (12 ounces), ends trimmed, cut on the diagonal into 2-inch pieces (about 2 cups)

½ small Fuji or Honeycrisp apple, very thinly sliced

2 tablespoons julienned fresh basil

1 scallion, finely chopped

1 tablespoon finely chopped fresh cilantro

1 tablespoon finely chopped fresh flat-leaf parsley

¼ cup crumbled feta cheese

Each spring I look forward to asparagus season and often consider how I'll incorporate the fiber-rich vegetable into my dishes. When they're finally available, I stock up, bunches at a time, before they're gone for the year. They pair well with grains, like farro, and with crisp apples and other veggies—exactly what this salad is all about. If you plan to prepare it ahead of time, set aside the herbs until ready to serve. For a heartier meal, top it with grilled chicken.

1 COOK THE FARRO: In a medium saucepan, combine 1 cup water and the salt. Bring to a boil over high heat, then stir in the farro. Turn the heat to medium-low, cover and cook until the grain is cooked but still a bit chewy, 18 to 20 minutes. (I like my farro with a nutty bite, but if you want the farro to be slightly softer, cook it longer, up to 25 minutes.) Drain and rinse with cold water. Let the farro cool while you make the rest of the salad.

2 MEANWHILE, MAKE THE DRESSING: In a small bowl, whisk together the lemon juice, olive oil, mustard, honey, salt, and pepper until blended. Set aside.

3 PREPARE THE REST OF THE SALAD: Fill a large bowl with water and ice. Fill a saucepan about halfway with water, stir in the salt, and bring to a boil over high heat. Add the snap peas and asparagus and cook for 2 minutes. Drain the vegetables and transfer them to the ice bath to stop the cooking. (You could also run them under ice-cold water, but it doesn't leave them quite as bright green.) When the vegetables are cool, drain again.

4 In a large salad bowl, combine the cooked farro, snap peas, asparagus, apple slices, basil, scallion, cilantro, and parsley and toss with the dressing. Add the feta and toss again to mix in the cheese just before serving.

TIPS FOR BUZY LIVES

Make It Ahead!

Since the cabbage is sturdy and holds up very well, this would be an excellent option for meal prepping. Just assemble the salad without dressing it. You can store it in the refrigerator, covered, up to 2 days. Keep the vinaigrette on the side and dress the salad as directed when you're ready to serve!

VIETNAMESE CHICKEN SALAD

SERVES 4   **TIME** 1 hour

FOR THE CHICKEN

½ cup sliced yellow onions

5 quarter-size slices peeled fresh ginger

2 bone-in, skin-on free-range chicken breasts (about 2 pounds total)

Kosher salt and freshly ground black pepper

FOR THE GINGER-LIME VINAIGRETTE

⅓ cup warm water

2 tablespoons sugar

2 tablespoons fish sauce

2 tablespoons lime juice

1 (2-inch) piece peeled fresh ginger, grated or finely minced

2 garlic cloves, finely minced

Chili-garlic sauce or sambal oelek (optional)

FOR THE SALAD

3 cups shredded green cabbage (from ½ medium head)

1 cup shredded red cabbage

½ cup shredded carrots

1 cup coarsely chopped fresh Vietnamese coriander (rau ram)

¼ cup coarsely chopped fresh mint

½ cup drained Quick Pickled Red Onions (page 198)

⅓ cup Fried Shallots (page 201) or canned fried onions

Now this is not another typical chicken salad. This Vietnamese classic is lighter, with peppery, minty notes, crunchy bites, and a tangy dressing. Many modern Vietnamese restaurants will have a version of this chicken salad, but when made at home, most households serve it with a side of chicken porridge, known as *chao ga*. (I have an easy *chao ga* recipe on my *Honeysuckle* YouTube channel.)

The chicken is the most crucial part of this salad. When you make it, traditionally, a chicken is boiled whole, but I find that risks drying out the meat too much. So I suggest steaming the chicken over gentle heat with onions and ginger to delicately infuse it with flavor. Try using free-range chicken, too, if you can, as its texture is more authentic.

---

1 COOK THE CHICKEN: Pour about 1 inch of water into a large saucepan or pot with a tight-fitting lid and set a steamer basket in the bottom (adjust the water level so it comes almost to the bottom of the basket). Bring the water to a boil. Carefully remove the insert and spread the onions and ginger inside it. Place the chicken breasts on top of the onions and ginger, skin-side up, and season generously with salt and pepper.

2 When the water comes to a boil, return the steamer insert with the chicken to the pot, cover, and reduce the heat to medium-low. (You want a gentle steam, not a hard steam.) Steam until the juices from the chicken run clear when you poke it with a skewer in the thickest part, about 20 minutes. Remove the chicken from the pot and set aside until cool enough to handle, 15 to 20 minutes. Remove the skin, pull the meat off the bones, and shred into different-size chunks.

3 WHILE THE CHICKEN COOKS, MAKE THE VINAIGRETTE: In a small bowl, whisk together the water, sugar, fish sauce, lime juice, ginger, and garlic to blend. If using chili-garlic sauce, add it to taste. Set aside for at least 10 minutes to let the flavors develop. (You can make the vinaigrette ahead of time and store it in the refrigerator, covered, for up to 1 week.)

4 ASSEMBLE THE SALAD: In a large bowl, combine the green cabbage, red cabbage, carrots, Vietnamese coriander, mint, pickled onions, and all the shredded chicken. Mix well to combine. Before serving, add about 3 tablespoons of the vinaigrette, mix well, and let it sit for about 10 minutes. (This will help soften the cabbage a bit.)

5 To serve, transfer the salad to a serving plate and top with fried shallots, then add vinaigrette to taste. Serve immediately.

CHILE-LIME STREET FRUIT SALAD

MAKES 4 servings   **TIME** 20 minutes

FOR THE TAJÍN DRESSING

½ cup extra-virgin olive oil

2 teaspoons lime juice

1 tablespoon Tajín

1 tablespoon honey

1 teaspoon finely chopped
fresh cilantro

1 teaspoon chili powder

1 teaspoon kosher salt

Freshly ground black pepper

FOR THE SALAD

6 ounces romaine lettuce,
chopped into ½-inch pieces

1 small jicama (about 8 ounces),
cut into ¼ × 2-inch matchsticks

1 mango, cut into small chunks

1 navel orange, peel cut
off with a knife, flesh cut into
half-moons

2 Persian (mini) cucumbers,
cut into ¼-inch-thick rounds

½ cup fresh jackfruit or canned
jackfruit in syrup (from a
20-ounce can), rinsed and
julienned

¼ cup grated or crumbled
Cotija cheese, plus more
for serving

⅓ cup toasted pumpkin seeds
(pepitas)

One of the first things I noticed after moving to Los Angeles were the bright, colorful fruit stands on the street corners, where they sell a variety of fresh tropical fruit on sticks or in bags, sprinkled with Tajín, a lime-spiked chile powder. Those flavors are refreshing and would harmonize well in a savory salad, perfect for the warm SoCal weather. Look for Tajín in the Hispanic foods section of any large or well-stocked grocery store.

1 MAKE THE TAJÍN DRESSING: In a small bowl, whisk together the olive oil, lime juice, Tajín, honey, cilantro, chili powder, salt, and black pepper to taste. Mix well and set aside for at least 15 minutes while you prepare the salad.

2 MAKE THE SALAD: Layer the romaine, jicama, mango, orange, cucumbers, and jackfruit in a large salad bowl. Top with the Cotija.

3 When ready to serve, mix the salad with the dressing and let it marinate for about 5 minutes to really let the fruits release their juices. (This will also help sweeten the salad dressing.) Sprinkle with more Cotija cheese and the toasted pumpkin seeds and serve.

FALL HARVEST SALAD

SERVES 4   **TIME** 35 minutes

FOR THE GOAT CHEESE

1 (4-ounce) log goat cheese

⅓ cup all-purpose flour

1 large egg, beaten

⅔ cup panko bread crumbs

1 teaspoon kosher salt

½ teaspoon garlic powder

FOR THE LEMON-BASIL DRESSING

2 tablespoons lemon juice

2 tablespoons extra-virgin olive oil

1 tablespoon minced fresh basil

2 teaspoons Dijon mustard

2 teaspoons honey

1 garlic clove, minced, or 1 teaspoon minced shallots

1 teaspoon kosher salt

Freshly ground black pepper

FOR THE SALAD

1 handful of green beans, trimmed and cut into 2-inch pieces (about 1 cup)

¼ cup extra-virgin olive oil

3 cups packed baby kale salad mix (about 3 ounces)

1 cup canned cannellini beans (about ½ can), rinsed and drained

1 carrot, sliced into ¼-inch discs

½ cup dried dates, halved, pitted, and sliced into ½-inch pieces

½ cup halved red grapes

1 Bosc pear, thinly sliced

½ cup store-bought candied walnuts

While I was growing up in the Bay Area, the valleys of Napa and Sonoma were just a quick weekend trip away for my family. I've celebrated many special occasions in the area—birthdays, engagement parties, and even our "mini-moon!" And when the leaves turn color, the shadows get longer, and the nights become crisper, there's nothing quite as magical as wine country.

This particular salad is inspired by a postcard vineyard view in Napa speckled with bright rustic hues. With fruity and savory cheese flavors, it's a hearty but easy meal for Indian summer.

1 **PREPARE THE GOAT CHEESE:** Slice the goat cheese log (see Note) into 5 roughly equal rounds.

2 **SET UP A DREDGING STATION:** Line a plate with waxed paper or parchment paper. Put the flour in one small bowl and the beaten egg in a second bowl. In a third bowl, stir together the panko, salt, and garlic powder. Working with one slice at a time, dip the goat cheese rounds first into flour to coat, then into the beaten egg, and then into the panko mixture, carefully coating each slice each time. Transfer the coated slices to the waxed paper and freeze for 15 minutes. (You can also make these ahead and simply refrigerate until ready to cook, up to 24 hours.)

3 **MAKE THE DRESSING:** In a small bowl, whisk together the lemon juice, olive oil, basil, mustard, honey, garlic, salt, and pepper to taste until the honey has dissolved. (You can make the dressing a day ahead of time and refrigerate until you're ready to use it.)

4 **PREPARE THE REST OF THE SALAD:** Bring a small saucepan with about 1 inch of water in it to a boil over high heat. Add the green beans and cook for 3 minutes, then drain and rinse with cold water to stop the cooking process. Set aside.

5 When you're ready to serve the salad, heat a large nonstick skillet over medium heat. Add the olive oil. When the oil is hot (a bit of panko should sizzle vigorously in the oil), add the chilled goat cheese slices and fry until golden brown on both sides, 2 to 3 minutes per side. Transfer the goat cheese to a plate lined with paper towels to drain for a moment.

6 In a large bowl, mix the baby kale with ¼ cup of the dressing. Transfer the kale to a large platter and arrange the green beans, cannellini beans, carrot, dates, grapes, pear, and walnuts on top.

7 Place the fried goat cheese over the arranged salad and drizzle the remaining dressing over the veggies and cheese just before serving.

Note Believe it or not, the easiest way to cut goat cheese is with unflavored dental floss, but you can also just use a thin knife.

SUMMER SUNSET SALAD

SERVES 2 to 4　**TIME** 30 minutes

2 ears yellow corn, shucked

FOR THE BASIL DRESSING

1 cup packed fresh basil leaves

¾ cup extra-virgin olive oil

¼ cup packed fresh flat-leaf parsley leaves

¼ cup lemon juice (from 2 lemons)

1 tablespoon grated Parmesan cheese

1 garlic clove, peeled

1 teaspoon Dijon mustard

1 teaspoon kosher salt

FOR THE SALAD

1 peach, cut into 6 wedges

1 fist-size heirloom tomato, cut into about 12 chunks

¼ cup roughly chopped fresh basil

2 avocados, cut into big bite-size chunks

2 cups packed baby arugula (about 2 ounces)

2 balls burrata cheese (6 to 8 ounces each)

After my career in finance I spent a few years working at *Sunset,* an iconic West Coast lifestyle magazine. I have such fond memories of working there and still keep close contact with many dear friends. Nate and I also got married on the magazine's beautiful campus, and we served a salad very much like this one to our guests. It's best made in the summer, to take advantage of the freshest produce: the sweet and crunchy corn, lusciously full peaches, and sun-ripened tomatoes. These ingredients shine together in this salad that can be prepared without spending too much time in a hot summer kitchen.

1 **FIRST, GRILL THE CORN:** Heat a gas or charcoal grill to medium heat (about 400°F). Brush the cooking grates clean. Add the corn and grill, turning occasionally, until the corn is charred in spots and bright yellow all over, 8 to 10 minutes. (You can also cook the corn in a pot of boiling water on the stove for 4 minutes, if you prefer.) Set aside until cool enough to handle.

2 **MAKE THE DRESSING:** In a food processor or blender, whirl together the basil, oil, parsley, lemon juice, Parmesan, garlic, mustard, and salt until green and smooth. Transfer the dressing to a bowl and set aside.

3 Place an ear of corn on a cutting board. Run a knife down one side of the cob to remove the kernels, then rotate the ear 90 degrees and repeat, cutting off another row of kernels, then keep turning the ear until all the kernels have been removed. Repeat with the second ear and transfer the kernels to a bowl.

4 **ASSEMBLE THE SALAD:** Add the peach, tomato, basil, and avocados to the bowl with the corn, along with ¼ cup of the vinaigrette, and stir gently until everything is coated. Arrange the arugula on a large platter. Spoon the mixture over the arugula and then nestle the burrata in the center of the salad. Spoon about 1 tablespoon of vinaigrette over each burrata, then serve immediately, with the extra vinaigrette on the side. Enjoy!

SPICY KOREAN CHICKEN STEW

SERVES 4 **TIME** 1 hour 30 minutes

1 (3.5-ounce) package of sweet potato noodles (dangmyeon), also called glass noodles

¼ cup gochujang

¼ cup soy sauce

¼ cup Korean soup soy sauce (guk ganjang)

2 teaspoons to 1 tablespoon gochugaru, to taste

2 tablespoons oyster sauce

2 tablespoons honey

4 garlic cloves, minced

1 tablespoon minced peeled fresh ginger

1 tablespoon sesame oil

1 tablespoon neutral-tasting oil (such as avocado oil)

1½ pounds boneless, skinless chicken thighs, quartered

4 cups low-sodium chicken broth

1 palm-size piece kombu (dried kelp)

1 large russet potato (about 1 pound), peeled and cut into 1-inch chunks

2 large carrots, cut into 1-inch chunks

½ onion, cut into thin wedges

Chopped scallions (green parts only), for garnish

Toasted sesame seeds, for garnish

White Rice (page 192), for serving

Kimchi, for serving

Nate and I were once watching a travel show about Seoul, South Korea, and the host tried a stew called *dakkjim*. It looked so incredible that I had to re-create it. After testing a few different recipes, I decided to make mine chunkier with slippery glass noodles for texture. The spice comes from both the gochugaru (Korean chile flakes) and gochujang (Korean chile paste), while Korean soup soy sauce (*guk ganjang*) deepens the seaweed-infused flavor. (Korean soup soy sauce is much saltier but lighter in color than your typical soy sauce, so be discerning.)

All the ingredients should be available at any large Asian market. The glass noodles are sometimes labeled as "sweet potato noodles," and appear thin, wiry, and translucent packed in bundles. You should find them in the dry noodles section.

1 Place the noodles in a large bowl, add warm water to cover, and set aside to soak until you need them.

2 In a small bowl, stir together the gochujang, soy sauce, soup soy sauce, gochugaru, oyster sauce, honey, garlic, ginger, and sesame oil until blended.

3 Heat a Dutch oven, soup pot, or large wok over medium-high heat. When hot, add the neutral oil, then the chicken, and cook the chicken until it is evenly cooked on the outside, 8 to 10 minutes, turning when it releases easily from the pan. Add the spicy soy sauce mixture, chicken broth, kombu, and 2 cups water. Bring to a boil, then reduce the heat to medium-low and simmer for 30 minutes, stirring occasionally. Remove the kombu.

4 Add the potato, carrots, and onion to the pot. Increase the heat to medium, cover, and simmer until the carrots are fork-tender, another 20 minutes or so.

5 Drain and add the noodles to the pot and let them cook until translucent and soft, another minute or so. Serve the stew garnished with scallions and toasted sesame seeds, with a side of kimchi.

TAKE IT FROM ME Add the Noodles Last

If you want to make the stew a day ahead but you want it to stay really brothy, soak and add the noodles to the soup as you reheat it the next day. The glass noodles soak up liquid and change texture overnight. It's still very good, but be aware that it becomes a much thicker, heartier type of dish.

HEALING MIRACLE SEAWEED SOUP (MIYEOK-GUK)

MAKES 4 to 6 servings   **TIME** 1 hour 45 minutes

5 garlic cloves

¼ pound rib-eye steak, cut into ½-inch pieces

1 tablespoon soy sauce

1 cup dried wakame seaweed

1 tablespoon sesame oil

2 tablespoons Korean soup soy sauce (guk ganjang), plus more for seasoning

Kosher salt

Aunt Gina is one of my very favorite people. She's technically Nate's aunt, and her sunny personality and loving support are such an inspiration to me. I always confide in her and seek her advice. We actually filmed most of our early *Honeysuckle* videos in her kitchen! While I was recovering after giving birth to Erisy, she brought me this special seaweed soup. With its healing power, it was the perfect medicine for my body. I learned this *miyeok-guk* is traditionally made in Korean culture on a child's birthday, to thank the mother for going through the pain of childbirth. Replenishing, hot, and nutritious, it's nothing short of a miracle. Make it for someone who needs a giant dose of love. The powers emerge after a long simmer, but it's pretty simple to put together.

You really don't need much beef for this, so ask your butcher to cut just a small part off a rib-eye steak, or buy a larger piece for the recipe and use the rest for Quicker Beef Pho (page 91). Serve it next to a steaming bowl of brown rice with a side of kimchi.

1 In a small bowl, mince 1 of the garlic cloves and mix it with the meat and soy sauce. Let the meat marinate for 30 minutes.

2 Meanwhile, put the seaweed in a bowl, add warm water to fill the bowl about halfway, and set aside to soak for 20 minutes. Drain the seaweed, cut it into bite-size pieces, then rinse the seaweed under warm water until clean, as needed. (Some seaweed comes perfectly clean already, but some brands can be a bit gritty, so use your judgment.)

3 Mince the remaining 4 garlic cloves. Heat a large pot over medium heat, then add the sesame oil and the minced garlic. Cook until fragrant, stirring, then add the marinated meat. Cook, stirring occasionally, until golden brown, about 3 minutes.

4 Add the chopped seaweed, soup soy sauce, and 8 cups water. Bring to a boil, then reduce the heat to medium-low, cover, and simmer for at least 1 hour (or longer). Season to taste with the soup soy sauce and serve hot. (You can let the soup cool and store it in the fridge, covered, up to 3 days. Reheat before serving.)

THREE BLENDED SOUPS

Simple blended soups are an amazing canvas for interesting toppings of all sorts. On their own, they're soothing and warming, but topped with a little crunch—say, in the form of hazelnuts and salty pieces of crisped prosciutto, or a dollop of crème fraîche—they're even more satisfying (and a little fancy). Best of all, the general technique is the same. You sauté some vegetables (I usually start with onions, celery, and carrots, otherwise known as a mirepoix), add your starring vegetable and just enough broth or stock to cover it, simmer until the vegetables are very soft, and blend away.

ROASTED TOMATO SOUP
SERVES 4   **TIME** 1 hour 30 minutes

2 pounds tomatoes, quartered

3 tablespoons extra-virgin olive oil

Kosher salt and freshly ground black pepper

½ medium onion, diced

1 carrot, chopped

2 garlic cloves, minced

1 (28-ounce) can crushed San Marzano tomatoes

¼ cup chopped fresh basil leaves

1 sprig fresh oregano

1 sprig fresh thyme

1 bay leaf

1½ cups vegetable broth

The classic combination of a grilled cheese sandwich and a rustic tomato soup is a standard and a definite favorite of mine. This recipe is my grown-up take on the nostalgic canned tomato soup, and it makes guests of all ages happy. When selecting ingredients, I always try to find vine-ripened tomatoes to roast for this soup. I think it's so rich and satisfying that you don't even need the cream often found in other tomato soup recipes!

1 Preheat the oven to 425°F. Line a rimmed baking sheet with foil.

2 Arrange the tomatoes skin-side up on the baking sheet, drizzle with 2 tablespoons of the olive oil, and season with salt and pepper. Roast for 30 minutes, or until the tomatoes are super juicy and beginning to brown.

3 When the tomatoes are done, in a medium soup pot, heat the remaining 1 tablespoon olive oil over medium heat. Add the onion and cook, stirring occasionally, until translucent, 2 to 3 minutes.

Add the carrot and garlic and cook for another 2 to 3 minutes, stirring every now and then, then add the roasted tomatoes (and any accumulated juices), the canned crushed tomatoes, the basil, oregano, thyme, bay leaf, and broth.

4 Simmer over medium-low heat for 40 minutes, stirring occasionally. Remove the herb stems and bay leaf, then blend with an immersion blender until smooth and add salt to taste. (You can let the soup cool and store it in the fridge, covered, up to 3 days. Reheat before serving.)

(recipe continues)

CAULIFLOWER SOUP

SERVES 4 to 6 **TIME** 45 minutes

2 tablespoons extra-virgin olive oil, plus more for serving

½ medium onion, diced

1 teaspoon kosher salt, plus more to taste

¼ teaspoon dried thyme

Dash of ground (or freshly grated) nutmeg

1 garlic clove, minced

5 cups chopped cauliflower (from half a 2-pound head)

1 medium Yukon Gold potato, chopped

3½ cups vegetable broth

Freshly ground black pepper

2 tablespoons chopped roasted hazelnuts

Crispy Prosciutto Chips (recipe follows)

1 tablespoon chopped fresh chives

Cauliflower is having a moment, finding its way into pizza crusts, gnocchi, and "rice" dishes. But it has always shined in soups. The base is simple, but adding the roasted hazelnuts and crispy prosciutto chips gives this soup some extra texture and flavors that will keep you coming back for more.

1 Heat a soup pot over medium-high heat, then add the olive oil and onion and cook until fragrant and just beginning to brown, stirring frequently, about 2 minutes. Stir in the salt, thyme, nutmeg, and garlic.

2 Add the cauliflower and potato, stir to blend, and add the vegetable broth. Bring to a boil, then reduce to a simmer, cover the pot, and simmer until the veggies are very soft, 15 to 20 minutes.

3 Blend the soup with an immersion blender until silky smooth, then season to taste with salt and pepper. (You can also add a little more vegetable broth or water here, if you'd prefer a thinner soup.)

4 To serve, ladle the soup into bowls. Garnish first with a drizzle of olive oil, then with a sprinkle of chopped hazelnuts, a few pieces of crisp prosciutto in the center, and a shower of chopped chives. Enjoy! (You can let the soup cool and store it in the fridge, covered, up to 3 days. Reheat before serving.)

CRISPY PROSCIUTTO CHIPS

MAKES about 1 cup **TIME** 15 minutes

4 slices prosciutto

These are delicious on soups or salads, or just eaten on their own as a treat.

1 Preheat the oven to 350°F. Line a baking sheet with parchment paper.

2 Place the prosciutto on the parchment and bake for 8 to 10 minutes, until crisp and golden brown. Remove from the oven and set aside to cool until you're ready to break them into shards and serve.

BUTTERNUT SQUASH SOUP
SERVES 4   **TIME** 1 hour

2 tablespoons extra-virgin olive oil

½ yellow onion, chopped

1 stalk celery, chopped

1 carrot, chopped

¼ teaspoon dried thyme

1 (2½-pound) butternut squash, peeled and cut into 1-inch pieces, or 2 pounds precut squash

1 large tart apple (such as Granny Smith or Honeycrisp), peeled and chopped

4 cups low-sodium chicken broth, plus more as needed

1½ teaspoons kosher salt, or to taste

¼ teaspoon ground (or freshly grated) nutmeg

¼ cup fresh flat-leaf parsley leaves

2 tablespoons crème fraîche

Ground white pepper

One of Erisy's first solid foods was pureed butternut squash. We were thrilled she loved it, but cooking separate things for a six-month-old baby and two tired adults was not a sustainable mode of operation. So I decided to use the leftover squash to make us soup. And believe me, we had a pretty steady diet of it for a few months—all the more reason to come up with a foolproof recipe. I like adding crème fraîche when serving, for a bit of creaminess. Yogurt also works, especially if you already have it in your fridge!

1 In a large Dutch oven, heat the olive oil over medium-high heat.

2 Add the onion and cook for a few minutes, stirring, until translucent. Add the celery, carrot, and thyme and continue to cook, stirring occasionally, until the vegetables are soft and golden brown, about 5 minutes. Add the squash, apple, chicken broth, salt, and nutmeg.

3 Bring to a boil, then reduce to a simmer and cook until the squash and apples are very soft, about 30 minutes.

4 Blend with an immersion blender and add salt to taste.

5 Serve the soup in bowls, garnished with parsley, crème fraîche, and a dusting of white pepper. (You can let the soup cool and store it in the fridge, covered, up to 3 days. Reheat before serving.)

QUICKER BEEF PHO

MAKES 4 servings **TIME** 50 minutes

FOR THE BROTH

1 yellow onion, halved

1 (4-inch) piece fresh ginger, halved lengthwise

1 black cardamom pod (see Note)

2 star anise

4 whole cloves

1 cinnamon stick

6 cups beef bone broth (see Note)

1 (2-inch) hunk rock sugar, or 1 tablespoon raw sugar

1 teaspoon kosher salt

2 tablespoons fish sauce, or to taste

FOR SERVING

1 (11-ounce) package dried ¼-inch-thick flat rice noodles (or a 16-ounce package fresh rice noodles for pad Thai)

¼ cup thinly sliced onion

¼ cup chopped fresh cilantro

¼ cup thinly sliced scallions (green parts only)

½ pound beef rib-eye steak (or other well-marbled beef), very thinly sliced

2 handfuls of mung bean sprouts (optional)

4 sprigs fresh Thai basil (optional)

1 jalapeño, sliced (optional)

Sriracha (optional)

Hoisin sauce (optional)

1 lime, cut into wedges, for serving

When I was growing up, my mom would make pho from scratch. For those who have not made pho before, it's an hours-long process, and she would spend the entire day cooking. Those were truly special and memorable meals. These days I'm often short on time, so I opt for a high-quality store-bought bone broth. It comes already slow-simmered so I still get that silky texture without sacrificing an entire day. Simmering the broth with all the right charred aromatics and spices, I'm transported straight back to my mother's kitchen.

1 **PREPARE THE BROTH:** Preheat your oven's broiler.

2 Place the onion and ginger on a baking sheet, cut-sides down. Broil for 10 to 15 minutes, until the outer layer is completely charred. (If you have a gas stove, you can char the onion and ginger directly over a high flame instead of broiling it.)

3 Meanwhile, in a medium soup pot over medium-high heat, toast the cardamom, star anise, cloves, and cinnamon stick until fragrant, about 2 minutes, stirring frequently, then remove from the heat. Transfer the small spices to a tea ball and put the tea ball in the pot, along with the cinnamon.

4 Add the charred onion and ginger to the pot, then add the broth, 6 cups water, the rock sugar, salt, and fish sauce. Bring to a boil, cook for 15 minutes, then remove the tea ball and cinnamon stick. Reduce

the heat and simmer for another 20 minutes to develop a rich, flavorful broth.

5 To prepare the noodles, while the broth cooks, bring another pot of water to a boil and cook the noodles according to package directions. I like to cook to serve as it keeps all the ingredients piping hot.

6 To make the onion mixture, in a small bowl, toss together the onion, cilantro, and scallions and set aside.

7 **TO SERVE:** Add the cooked noodles to a bowl, top with raw beef, and garnish with a bit of the onion mixture. Leaving the onions and ginger in the pot, ladle the boiling broth directly over the meat so it cooks, and serve the pho immediately with optional garnishes as desired: bean sprouts, Thai basil leaves, lime, and jalapeño slices. Add sriracha and hoisin sauce, as you prefer.

Notes Black cardamom lends a unique smoky flavor to the broth, but it can be hard to find. Look online or skip it if you must, but don't substitute green cardamom, because it really doesn't have the same flavor.

If you can't find bone broth (I often buy the kind sold in the freezer section), use 8 cups low-sodium beef broth and just 4 cups water.

VIETNAMESE CRAB NOODLE SOUP (BÚN RIÊU)

MAKES 4 to 6 servings   TIME 45 minutes

FOR THE RIÊU (PORK AND CRAB MIXTURE)

3 large eggs

¼ cup spicy crab paste seasoning

12 ounces lump crabmeat, freshly cooked or canned (about 1½ cups)

¼ pound ground pork

1 garlic clove, minced

Salt and freshly ground black pepper

FOR THE BROTH

2 tablespoons neutral-tasting oil (such as avocado oil)

1 teaspoon annatto seeds

1 garlic clove, minced

¼ cup chopped onion

3 Roma (plum) tomatoes, quartered

8 cups low-sodium chicken broth

½ teaspoon sugar

1 teaspoon fish sauce

12 ounces fried tofu cubes, cut into 1 inch chunks

(ingredients continue)

Bún riêu is a soupy mix of noodles, crabmeat, egg, pork, and, nowadays, tofu. The egg mixture floats to the soup's surface like a pillowy cloud. Like many other Vietnamese soups, *bún riêu* invites an array of fresh toppings. My parents liked to add shredded water spinach (*rau muon*), which my sister and I had to laboriously prepare, sitting on the floor with a special shredding tool. I still get nightmares thinking about how much we had to cut—enough for all our nearby relatives. So now I use shiso instead! I also shortcut with store-bought spicy crab paste, which is made with tamarind, soy, tomato paste, and other robust spices. This is a crucial ingredient, so make sure you look for it in the soup mix aisle of a good Asian market.

Once you start cooking, the soup comes together really quickly—just cook the noodles first so they're ready when the soup is done. (See Rice Noodle Tips, page 113.) Look for brown-skinned fried tofu, sold in either blocks or cubes, in the tofu section of an Asian market. Traditionally, we add shrimp paste (sometimes labeled "fine shrimp sauce") and chili-garlic sauce for extra flavor at the end.

1 **MAKE THE RIÊU:** In a small bowl, whisk the eggs to blend, then stir in the crab paste until well blended. Add the crabmeat, pork, garlic, and a dash each of salt and pepper and stir until the pork is evenly distributed. Set aside.

2 **MAKE THE BROTH:** In a medium pot, heat the oil over medium heat. Add the annatto seeds and fry for 3 to 4 minutes to extract their flavor. Using a large spoon, carefully remove and discard all of the seeds. Add the garlic and onion to the oil and cook, stirring, for about a minute. Add the tomatoes and cook until they start to get tender, another 3 to 4 minutes. Add the chicken broth and bring the soup to a boil. When the tomatoes float to the top, begin adding the *riêu* mixture in large spoonfuls (about 2 tablespoons per spoonful). Once you've added all of it, cook for about a minute, undisturbed, so the *riêu* mixture floats to the top of the liquid. Add the sugar and fish sauce and give the soup a very gentle stir. Add the tofu chunks, cover, and remove from the heat.

(recipe continues)

FOR SERVING

¼ cup thinly sliced onion

¼ cup chopped fresh cilantro

¼ cup thinly sliced scallions
(green parts only)

1 (14-ounce) package dried
round vermicelli (rice noodles,
sometimes labeled bún giang
tay), cooked according to
package directions

2 cups sliced green leaf lettuce

2 handfuls of mung bean sprouts

½ cup finely sliced shiso leaves

1 lime, cut into wedges

Shrimp paste

Chili-garlic sauce

3 TO SERVE: In a small bowl, toss together the onion, cilantro, and scallions. Divide the vermicelli among four to six large bowls and garnish with a little bit of the onion mixture. Ladle the soup mixture over the noodles. Serve immediately, garnished with lettuce, bean sprouts, shiso leaves, and lime juice. Add shrimp paste and chili-garlic sauce to taste. Enjoy! (This is best eaten the same day.)

Note You can cook the noodles while the broth simmers, or you can complete the soup, keep it warm over the lowest heat setting, and cook the noodles just before eating—whatever seems easier for you.

CHICKEN, LEMON, AND HERB NOODLE SOUP

SERVES 2 to 4   **TIME** 45 minutes

2 tablespoons extra-virgin olive oil

1 pound boneless, skinless chicken thighs, cut into 1-inch chunks

Kosher salt and freshly ground black pepper

1 cup diced onion

2 stalks celery, chopped

2 carrots, chopped

1 garlic clove, minced

½ teaspoon dried thyme

6 cups low-sodium chicken broth

1½ cups bow tie pasta

1 sprig fresh rosemary

1 tablespoon chopped fresh dill

Juice of ½ lemon (about 2 tablespoons), plus more to taste

Chopped fresh flat-leaf parsley, for serving

Whenever I get sick, there's only one thing that I crave: a hearty bowl of chicken noodle soup. My dad used to stock up on canned soups for whenever my sister or I got sick, because it was easy, and sure enough, it did the job. I no longer default to canned soup because I enjoy this made from-scratch, lemony herb one so much more! The brightness of the lemons gives off a punch of freshness, which—trust me—helps when you're feeling under the weather. And the herbs elevate and round out the broth.

Keep in mind that you don't have to limit yourself to just dill and parsley; any fresh herbs like basil, chives, and tarragon would also be delicious here, so use what you have or what you like best.

1 Heat a heavy-bottomed pot or Dutch oven over medium-high heat. When hot, add the olive oil and the chicken thighs, and season well with salt and pepper. Cook, turning occasionally once the chicken releases easily from the pan, until the chicken is golden brown on all sides, about 5 minutes. Transfer the chicken to a bowl, leaving the juices in the pot.

2 Reduce the heat to medium, add the onion, and cook until the onion is translucent, 3 to 5 minutes. Add the celery, carrots, garlic, and thyme. Cook and stir until the vegetables have softened, another 5 minutes. Add the chicken broth,

scraping any browned bits off the bottom of the pot with a wooden spoon. Return the chicken (and any accumulated juices) to the pot, bring to a boil, and cook another 5 minutes.

3 Add the pasta, rosemary, dill, and lemon juice. Simmer over medium-high heat just until the pasta is al dente, about 12 minutes. Season to taste with salt, pepper, and more lemon, if desired, then serve with a sprinkle of parsley. (You can let the soup cool and store it in the fridge, covered, up to 5 days. Keep the pasta separate and add more broth when reheating. Reheat before serving.) Enjoy!

VIETNAMESE VEGETARIAN TAMARIND SOUP (CANH CHUA CHAY)

MAKES 4 servings **TIME** 45 minutes

1 tablespoon extra-virgin olive oil

2 garlic cloves, minced

1 shallot, finely chopped

2 vine or Roma (plum) tomatoes, cut into sixths

2 (½-inch-thick) rings fresh pineapple, cut into chunks (about 1 cup)

10 okra pods, cut on the diagonal into ½-inch pieces (about 1 cup)

2 tablespoons dark brown sugar

2 tablespoons soy sauce

1 tablespoon mushroom powder or umami powder

Kosher salt

4 cups vegetable broth

½ cup tamarind paste, store-bought or homemade (see below)

1 stalk bac ha (also known as elephant ear or taro stem), thin skin peeled, cut on the diagonal into 1-inch pieces (about 2 cups)

1 cup fresh jackfruit or canned jackfruit in syrup (from half a 20-ounce can), rinsed, each piece shredded into thirds

Freshly ground black pepper

1 cup mung bean sprouts

2 tablespoons chopped ngo om (also known as rice paddy herb), Thai basil, or cilantro, for garnish

You may not have heard of it until now, but this traditional catfish- or shrimp-filled soup, sometimes served with Vietnamese Caramelized Fish (page 147), is a quintessential Vietnamese dish. We had this on a weekly basis growing up, either at home or at the temple, usually vegetarian style. My dad even grew his own taro stem plant (also called "elephant ear," or *bac ha* in Vietnamese) in the backyard, so they'd have the star ingredient at the ready. I love how the sweet pineapple and tomato balance the sour tamarind and savory soup base. A whirlwind of flavors, this soup will open all your taste buds.

Bac ha can be challenging to find if you don't have access to a good Vietnamese or Asian market. If you can't find it, you can always substitute 1 cup rinsed canned bamboo shoots or sliced celery. Same goes for the *ngo om*, or "rice paddy herb"—it has an amazing flavor, but you can use Thai basil or cilantro instead.

1 Heat a large soup pot over medium heat. When hot, add the olive oil, garlic, and shallot. Let them cook, stirring occasionally, until fragrant and golden brown, about 2 minutes. Add the tomatoes and pineapple and cook until softened, another 2 to 3 minutes. Add the okra, brown sugar, soy sauce, mushroom powder, and 2 teaspoons salt and mix for about a minute.

2 Add the vegetable broth, 1 cup water, and the tamarind paste, then bring the soup to a rapid boil. Reduce the heat to a simmer and let cook for about 10 minutes just to cook the vegetables. (At this point you can turn the soup off and let it sit, covered, for an hour or two, if you want.)

3 Once you're ready to serve, bring the soup back up to a boil and add the *bac ha* and jackfruit. Let the soup cook for about 3 minutes to warm the ingredients through, season to taste with salt and pepper, and then transfer it to a large bowl. Serve with bean sprouts (I like to chop mine in half for easier serving) and sprinkle with *ngo om*. Serve immediately.

TAKE IT FROM ME DIY Tamarind Paste

While you can buy jars of tamarind paste, I find that making it myself is easy, tastes better, and costs less. Start with a big block of seedless tamarind pulp, available at most Asian markets. Pull off about 2 tablespoons from the tamarind block and place it in a bowl with ½ cup hot water. Let it stand until the tamarind is soft, about 15 minutes. Pour the tamarind and the water mixture into a fine mesh sieve over a bowl and use a spoon to push the pulp through the sieve. Be sure to scrape the paste off the underside of the sieve. Mix the strained pulp well to make a thin paste. Discard the fibers and use the paste as needed.

HOT AND SOUR SOUP

SERVES 2 to 4   **TIME** 25 minutes

½ cup dried sliced shiitake mushrooms (from half a 1-ounce package)

1 cup hot water

2 tablespoons cornstarch

1 teaspoon sesame oil

1 teaspoon grated peeled fresh ginger

1 garlic clove, minced

3 medium cremini mushrooms, thinly sliced (about ½ cup)

¼ cup sliced bamboo shoots, cut into ¼-inch-wide strips

4 cups low-sodium chicken broth

4 ounces extra-firm tofu, sliced into 1-inch-long matchsticks

2 tablespoons rice vinegar

1 tablespoon soy sauce

1 teaspoon kosher salt

1 teaspoon chili-garlic sauce, or to taste

1 large egg, whisked to blend

Sliced scallions (green parts only), for serving

Ground white pepper (also called white pepper powder) or freshly ground black pepper, for serving

I appreciate the convenience of takeout, but there are some dishes that just don't compare to homemade. Hot and sour soup is an excellent example, and it's ready faster than the time it takes to haul home that packaged takeout. But don't make it so quickly that you miss the beautiful egg ribbons forming as they're cooked in the soup; the cooking process is the real performance to watch. This soup can be as spicy as you'd like, depending on how much pepper and chili-garlic sauce you add. Feel free to add pork or other vegetables along with the cremini mushrooms or tofu, as specified in the directions below.

1 Put the shiitake mushrooms in a bowl and add the hot water to cover. Set aside for 10 minutes to rehydrate, then move the mushrooms to a bowl and transfer ¼ cup of the mushroom-soaking liquid to another small bowl. Add the cornstarch to the liquid, stir to blend, and set aside.

2 Heat a large soup pot over medium-high heat. Add the sesame oil, ginger, and garlic and cook until fragrant, stirring frequently, about 2 minutes. Add the reserved shiitake mushrooms, the cremini mushrooms, and bamboo shoots. Cook for another 2 minutes, stirring frequently to prevent the garlic from getting too brown.

3 Add the chicken broth and tofu and bring the soup to a boil. Reduce the heat and simmer, stirring occasionally, until all the mushrooms are cooked, 10 to 12 minutes.

4 Add the vinegar, soy sauce, kosher salt, and chili-garlic sauce. Whisk the cornstarch mixture again, then add it to the soup, stirring until the soup thickens. Finally, while stirring the soup gently, drizzle in the whisked egg, which will cook on contact and form little ribbons in the soup. Serve piping hot, with sliced scallions and ground white pepper to taste. (You can let the soup cool and store it in the fridge, covered, up to 3 days. Reheat before serving.)

TORTELLINI E FAGIOLE

SERVES 4 to 6   **TIME** 1 hour 15 minutes

¼ cup extra-virgin olive oil

½ large yellow onion, chopped

3 slices thick-cut bacon, chopped

4 garlic cloves, finely chopped

2 stalks celery, finely chopped

2 carrots, finely chopped

2 teaspoons Italian seasoning (or a mixture of dried basil, thyme, rosemary, oregano, and/or marjoram)

1 (14.5-ounce) can diced tomatoes

1 (8-ounce) can tomato sauce

1 teaspoon sugar

4 cups low-sodium beef broth

1 bay leaf

1 (15-ounce) can cannellini beans, rinsed and drained

1 (roughly 3-inch) rind of Parmesan cheese (optional)

2 cups fresh or frozen cheese tortellini (from an 8-ounce package)

2 cups chopped curly or lacinato kale, stems discarded

¼ cup fresh flat-leaf parsley, chopped

Kosher salt and freshly ground black pepper

Parmesan cheese, for serving

The best job I had in college was working at a local pasta restaurant. My favorite break-time soup was a beef and spinach tortellini soup, because I was enamored with its cheesy parts, but also its green bits, too. I've also always loved classic pasta e fagiole, a traditional Italian soup with small pasta and beans. I discovered a way to mash these both together to make a super-soup. I make pasta e fagiole with tortellini instead of the pasta, then throw in some bacon for richness (without getting too heavy) and a Parmesan rind (for deep, cheesy flavor that rounds out the soup). The leafy greens also help keep things light, and it all tastes amazing after a few hours of simmering on the stove. Of course, if you don't have that much time, it's still foolproof after an hour.

1 In a Dutch oven or heavy-bottomed pot, heat the olive oil over medium-high heat. Add the onion and cook, stirring, until fragrant, about 2 minutes. Add the bacon and continue to cook until the bacon begins to brown and crisp, about 3 minutes. Reduce the heat to medium and add the garlic, celery, carrots, and Italian seasoning. Cook, stirring occasionally, until the vegetables soften, another 5 minutes.

2 Add the diced tomatoes, tomato sauce, sugar, beef broth, 1 cup water, the bay leaf, and half of the cannellini beans. (If you're using a Parmesan rind, add that now, too.) Simmer over medium-low heat for 45 minutes, stirring occasionally.

3 Add the remaining cannellini beans, the tortellini, and kale. Simmer until the tortellini are cooked through, about 15 minutes for fresh, 25 minutes for frozen. Remove the Parmesan rind. Stir in the parsley and season to taste with salt and pepper. Serve the soup with fresh shavings of Parmesan cheese. (You can let the soup cool and store it in the fridge, covered, up to 3 days. Reheat before serving.)

SALMON AND CORN CHOWDER

SERVES 3 or 4 **TIME** 1 hour

1 tablespoon plus 2 teaspoons extra-virgin olive oil

1 (8-ounce) salmon fillet (about 1 inch thick)

3 slices bacon, chopped into ½-inch pieces

½ medium onion, diced

1 medium carrot, diced

1 stalk celery, diced

½ teaspoon dried thyme

2 garlic cloves, minced

2 tablespoons all-purpose flour

1½ teaspoons kosher salt, plus more to taste

1 teaspoon Old Bay seasoning

1 teaspoon paprika

½ teaspoon dried basil

1 cup half-and-half, warmed

4 cups low-sodium chicken broth

2 cups fresh corn kernels (from 2 ears)

3 medium Yukon Gold potatoes (about 1 pound), peeled and cut into ½-inch cubes (about 2 cups)

Freshly ground black pepper

Chopped scallions (green parts only), for serving

Oyster crackers, for serving

Every coastal region in America has a proud local chowder (or "chowdah"). My region is San Francisco. Whenever I went to Fisherman's Wharf, I'd treat myself to a large clam chowder served in a round sourdough bread bowl. Summers in San Francisco are gray and can feel like winter, so clam chowders work well there, but now that I'm in LA, something lighter like my salmon and seasonal corn chowder is more appropriate. Serve this with a glass of chilled white wine and it's one of the best late summer meals.

1 Heat a small skillet over medium-high heat. When hot, drizzle 2 teaspoons of the olive oil around the pan, add the salmon, skin-side down, and cook until the skin is golden brown and releases easily from the pan, about 4 minutes. Flip the salmon over and continue cooking for another 4 minutes. Transfer the salmon to a plate to cool.

2 Meanwhile, heat a medium Dutch oven over medium heat, then drizzle in the remaining 1 tablespoon olive oil and add the bacon. Cook, stirring occasionally, until the bacon begins to brown, about 3 minutes. Add the onion and cook, stirring, until the onion is translucent, about 3 minutes. Add the carrot, celery, thyme, and garlic. Cook until the vegetables are soft, another

3 to 5 minutes. Add the flour, salt, Old Bay, paprika, and basil. Cook for another minute or so, then slowly add the half-and-half, stirring the veggies well as you add it so that there's no clumping. After the mixture thickens and bubbles again, add the chicken broth, corn, and potatoes. Bring to a boil, reduce the heat to medium-low, and simmer, stirring occasionally, until the potatoes are tender throughout, about 20 minutes.

3 Remove the skin from the salmon, break it into bite-size chunks, add it to the pot, and simmer for another 5 minutes. Season to taste with salt and pepper. Serve garnished with scallions and oyster crackers. (You can let the soup cool and store it in the fridge, covered, up to 3 days. Reheat before serving.)

TIPS FOR BUZY LIVES The Tool to Get.

While it doesn't take all that long to cut corn kernels off the cob, you can definitely substitute frozen corn for fresh. But if there's one kitchen gadget to get, it's the Oxo corn prep peeler; it's an amazing tool that gets the job done in no time.

New Favorites
NOODLES + GRAINS

Noodles and grains are common staples in most households. I personally look forward to our weekly pasta nights, not just for the noodles, but because it means that Nate is cooking. Noodles can also be made into fancier meals. In this chapter you'll find some tasty ways to use a fun variety of noodles and grains in both familiar and unexpected ways.

GARLIC NOODLES *with* CRAB

SERVES 4   **TIME** 30 minutes

1 pound fresh wheat noodles, knife cut, or spaghetti pasta

1 tablespoon soy sauce

1 tablespoon oyster sauce

1 tablespoon fish sauce

1 tablespoon sugar

2 tablespoons extra-virgin olive oil

2 tablespoons unsalted butter

6 garlic cloves, minced

¼ onion, sliced

8 ounces lump crabmeat, freshly cooked or canned (about 1 cup)

½ teaspoon Cajun seasoning

½ teaspoon smoked paprika

Coarsely ground black pepper

2 scallions (green parts only), sliced, for serving

There's an iconic upscale Vietnamese fusion restaurant in San Francisco known for their famous roasted crab, served with a side of garlic noodles, which are from a top-secret recipe. The bouncy, buttery, flavor-spiked mouthfuls really kept us coming back for more. When I tried to re-create the dish at home, I started with fresh noodles, added crabmeat, and experimented with Cajun seasoning and smoked paprika. It was a hit! Now we have a new take on the famous pairing—and it's easy enough for weeknights.

1 Cook the noodles to al dente according to package directions. Drain and rinse well with cold water to remove any excess starch.

2 Meanwhile, in a small bowl, mix together the soy sauce, oyster sauce, fish sauce, sugar, and 1 tablespoon water to blend. Set the sauce aside.

3 In a large skillet or wok, heat 1 tablespoon each of the olive oil and butter over medium-high heat. Add one-third of the minced garlic and cook, stirring, for about a minute. Add the onion and stir-fry until the garlic just begins to brown, about another minute. Add the crab, Cajun seasoning, smoked paprika, and pepper to taste. Cook for another minute, stirring to combine the flavors. Transfer to a bowl and set aside.

4 Return the skillet to medium heat and add the remaining 1 tablespoon each olive oil and butter. Add the remaining minced garlic and cook until fragrant, 1 to 2 minutes. (You want it to get nice and tanned but not burnt.) Add the sauce, let it sizzle for a second, then add the cooked noodles. Mix well with tongs for 2 to 3 minutes to coat all the noodles with the sauce, then add about one-quarter of the crab mixture and stir for another minute or so to warm through.

5 Transfer the noodles to a serving bowl or platter and top with the rest of the crab. Garnish with the scallions and a bit more ground pepper. (This is best eaten the same day.)

TAKE IT FROM ME A Side Dish Option

If you want to serve this as a hearty side dish instead, just leave out the onions, crab, smoked paprika, and Cajun seasoning. Swap those out for a hefty sprinkle of Parmesan cheese on top of the noodles.

BULGOGI JAPCHAE

SERVES 4 to 6 **TIME** 40 minutes, plus marinating time

¼ cup sugar

⅓ cup soy sauce

2 tablespoons sesame oil

1 bunch spinach (about 7 ounces)

8 ounces sweet potato noodles (dangmyeon), also called glass noodles

1 tablespoon avocado oil

1 medium carrot, cut into 2-inch matchsticks

½ red bell pepper, thinly sliced

3 scallions (green parts only), chopped into 3-inch sections

½ yellow onion, sliced

4 medium fresh shiitake mushrooms, sliced, stems discarded (about ½ cup)

3 garlic cloves, minced

About 2 cups Quick Bulgogi (recipe follows)

One of the many YouTube videos we filmed in Aunt Gina's kitchen was the *japchae* recipe, a classic Korean sweet potato noodle stir-fry with marinated beef bulgogi and vegetables, which can be eaten warm or cold and served as a side dish for a larger Korean feast or enjoyed on its own. My version starts with a flavorful bulgogi, which is itself a shortcut recipe and can be made in a pinch. This Bulgogi Japchae tastes authentic enough that it even won Nate's *halmoni*'s (Korean grandmother) approval.

1 In a small bowl, whisk together the sugar, soy sauce, and sesame oil to blend. Set aside.

2 Fill a medium bowl with ice and water. Fill a large pot about three-quarters of the way with water and bring to a boil. Add the spinach to the boiling water, let cook for about 15 seconds, then transfer the spinach to the ice water. (Keep the boiling water on the stove.) Let the spinach cool for about 10 seconds, then drain. Squeeze the excess water out of the spinach with your hands. Roughly chop the spinach and set aside.

3 Add the sweet potato noodles to the boiling water and cook until soft, 3 to 5 minutes. (Certain brands take longer, so cook according to the package directions.) Drain and set aside.

4 Heat a large well-seasoned cast-iron or nonstick skillet over medium-high heat. Add the avocado oil, then add the carrot, bell pepper, scallions, onion, mushrooms, and garlic and stir to coat. Stir-fry until they start to soften, about 3 minutes. Add the spinach and noodles and stir for a minute or so, until the vegetables are incorporated into the noodle mixture, then add the soy sauce mixture and toss with tongs (or even your hands!) to coat all the ingredients. Finally, add the bulgogi and mix again until the meat is well distributed. Serve hot or cold! Finished *japchae* can be refrigerated for up to 3 days and reheated.

(recipe continues)

QUICK BULGOGI

MAKES about 4 cups   **TIME** 15 minutes, plus marinating time

¼ cup soy sauce

2 tablespoons sesame oil

1 tablespoon light brown sugar

2 tablespoons honey

3 garlic cloves, minced

1 pound beef (such as rib-eye or sirloin), very thinly sliced (see below)

½ medium yellow onion, cut into 1-inch chunks

1 tablespoon toasted sesame seeds

4 tablespoons avocado oil, or as needed

This Korean classic, a stir-fried marinated beef dish that normally sits for hours to soak up flavor, is the perfect addition to *japchae*, but it's also great over a simple bowl of rice (which is why I always like to make double what I need for the *japchae*). I like using my hands to make sure every piece of beef gets evenly coated with the sauce before it marinates. Before you start, read Buying Sliced Beef (see below).

1   In a large bowl, stir together the soy sauce, sesame oil, brown sugar, honey, and garlic. Add the beef, peeling the slices apart as you put them into the bowl. Add the onion and sesame seeds and stir until all the beef pieces are well coated. Cover the bowl with plastic wrap and marinate, refrigerated, for 1 to 5 hours.

2   When ready to cook, heat a large skillet over medium-high heat. When hot, add 2 tablespoons of the oil, then add about one-third of the meat and onion mixture and cook, stirring occasionally, until the meat is cooked through on all sides and the onion has softened, about 3 minutes.

3   Transfer the meat to a bowl. Repeat to cook two more batches of meat, adding an additional tablespoon of oil (or as needed) to the pan before each batch. Serve immediately, or use in Bulgogi Japchae (page 107). Allow any leftover beef to cool and refrigerate, covered, for up to 3 days.

TIPS FOR BUZY LIVES Buying Sliced Beef

If you want tender, authentic bulgogi, you need to start with very thinly sliced beef. If you want, you can slice your own: Purchase your own rib-eye or sirloin steak, then freeze it for about 30 minutes, and it will be easier to slice than straight out of the refrigerator. But because I like my meat sliced super thin, I always purchase it at an Asian market. Look for meat labeled "for shabu shabu" or "for barbecue."

CHICKEN CHOW MEIN

SERVES 4 **TIME** 25 minutes

FOR THE SAUCE

¼ cup oyster sauce

2 tablespoons soy sauce

1 tablespoon plus 1 teaspoon sesame oil

2 teaspoons light brown sugar

Freshly ground black pepper

FOR THE NOODLES

1 (14-ounce) package fresh chow mein noodles, fresh ramen, or yakisoba noodles

2 tablespoons avocado oil or coconut oil

3 boneless, skinless chicken thighs (about ¾ pound total), cut into ½-inch-thick strips

¼ teaspoon kosher salt

3 garlic cloves, minced

1 teaspoon grated peeled fresh ginger

1 medium carrot, cut on the diagonal into ¼-inch-thick rounds

1 large stalk celery, cut on the diagonal into ¼-inch-thick slices

½ medium yellow onion, sliced

2 scallions (green parts only), cut into 2-inch pieces

2 baby bok choy, cut on the diagonal into 1-inch-thick pieces

Chopped fresh cilantro, for garnish

Whenever we go to a Chinese restaurant, Nate pretends to carefully study the menu, but he always orders the chow mein. Even at some Vietnamese places, he'll ask if they serve chow mein (a slightly different style than the Chinese version). And I get it—it's a comforting, hot stir-fry with salty noodles and meat. I find it's a great dish to stuff with crunchy veggies as well. Toss everything up in a sizzling hot wok and dinner is done.

An Asian market is the best place to find chow mein noodles—just look for the words "steamed chow mein" on the package, and make sure they're made with eggs. Fresh noodles have the best structure—especially when you steam them instead of boiling them, which prevents them from getting mushy. If you can't find chow mein noodles, it's okay to substitute other types of noodles, such as dried ramen or soba noodles.

1 **MAKE THE SAUCE:** In a small bowl, whisk together the oyster sauce, soy sauce, sesame oil, brown sugar, and ¼ cup water. Season with pepper to taste, then whisk together until the sugar dissolves. Set the sauce aside.

2 **PREPARE THE NOODLES:** Pour an inch or two of water into a large pot with a tight-fitting lid and set a steamer basket in the bottom (adjust the water level so it comes almost to the bottom of the basket). Bring the water to a boil, then add the noodles and steam until softened but still slightly undercooked, 3 to 5 minutes. Transfer the noodles to a bowl and set aside.

3 Heat a large wok over high heat. When hot, add the avocado oil. Once the oil starts to smoke, add the chicken and season with the salt. Cook for 2 minutes, stirring, then add the garlic and ginger. Continue cooking and stirring until the chicken is cooked through and lightly browned on all sides, another 2 to 3 minutes. Add the carrot, celery, onion, scallions, and bok choy and cook until the vegetables start to soften, about 3 minutes. (They should still have a slight crunch.) Add the noodles and sauce and cook, mixing everything together thoroughly as you go (tongs work great here), until the noodles are soft, the sauce has been absorbed, and the vegetables are evenly distributed, another 3 minutes. (If you want the noodles to be saucier, add 2 tablespoons water.)

4 Serve hot, garnished with cilantro. Store any uneaten noodles in the refrigerator, covered, and reheat in a nonstick skillet with a splash of water over medium heat.

VIETNAMESE GRILLED PORK NOODLE SALAD

SERVES 4 to 6   **TIME** 50 minutes, plus marinating time

FOR THE PORK

2 tablespoons sugar

2 tablespoons fish sauce

2 tablespoons thick soy sauce, or 2 tablespoons regular soy sauce plus 2 teaspoons molasses

2 tablespoons extra-virgin olive oil

2 tablespoons minced lemongrass

2 tablespoons minced shallots

¼ teaspoon sesame oil

Kosher salt and freshly ground black pepper

1½ pounds pork shoulder, sliced into 2 × 3-inch strips about ⅛ inch thick

FOR THE SALAD

1 pound dried rice vermicelli (size S)

Neutral-tasting oil (such as avocado oil), for cooking the pork

4 cups shredded green leaf or romaine lettuce

2 cups mung bean sprouts

¼ cup finely chopped fresh mint

¼ cup finely chopped fresh cilantro

¼ cup finely chopped fresh shiso leaves

1 small English cucumber, shredded

1⅓ cups drained Pickled Carrots and Daikon (page 198)

¼ cup chopped roasted peanuts

½ cup Scallion Relish (page 201)

Fish Sauce Vinaigrette (recipe follows), for serving

After pho and bánh mì, noodle salad is one of the most popular Vietnamese dishes today. It's a common street food in Vietnam and ideal for a light lunch on a scorching hot day. The cold rice noodles topped with fresh vegetables and herbs, all coated in a sweet and tangy sauce, and sometimes served with grilled shrimp, egg rolls, or grilled tofu, make for an explosive flavor combination. Often when my mom or grandma said they were too lazy to cook anything, they'd quickly throw this together for us. (Given that the meat tastes best if it's marinated for at least 4 hours, it's not exactly my definition of an instant dinner, but I think they defined "quick" differently back then!) If you're looking to save time, I recommend using presliced shabu shabu or Korean marinated pork instead. You'll need eight 12-inch bamboo skewers for grilling the pork.

1 **MARINATE THE PORK:** In a large bowl, whisk together the sugar, fish sauce, thick soy sauce, olive oil, lemongrass, shallots, sesame oil, and salt and pepper to taste. Using your hands or a spatula, mix the pork until evenly coated with the sauce. Cover and refrigerate for at least 4 hours, or overnight.

2 About an hour before you plan to cook, soak eight 12-inch bamboo skewers in a pan of water to prevent them from burning on the grill.

3 **PREPARE THE SALAD:** Cook the noodles according to package directions. Drain the noodles, rinse well with cold water, and set aside to drain in the sieve.

4 Heat a gas or charcoal grill to medium heat (about 400°F). Thread the pork onto the skewers, dividing the meat evenly among them. Brush the cooking grates clean and rub with oil, then place the pork skewers over direct heat and grill, covered, until cooked through, 5 to 7 minutes on each side. (Alternatively, you could cook the pork in a large cast-iron skillet: Heat the skillet over medium-high heat, then add 2 teaspoons neutral oil. Add as many pork pieces as will fit in a single layer, spreading them across the pan and taking care not to overcrowd them. Cook, stirring, until browned and cooked through, 4 to 5 minutes. Transfer to a plate, scraping the lemongrass out of the pan along with the pork. Repeat with the remaining pork, adding more oil as needed, until all the pork is cooked.)

(recipe continues)

5 When ready to serve, dividing evenly, fill each of four bowls with the lettuce, bean sprouts, mint, cilantro, and shiso and mix to blend. (For smaller servings, you can stretch it across six bowls.) Divide the noodles, cucumber, and pickled carrots and daikon among the bowls. Add the pork (you can remove the pork from the skewers, or add the skewers of pork to each for presentation). Sprinkle the pork with peanuts and top the noodles with the scallion relish. Serve immediately, with a side of the fish sauce vinaigrette, for drizzling over the top.

FISH SAUCE VINAIGRETTE (NUOC MAM CHAM)

MAKES 1½ cups **TIME** 5 minutes

⅔ cup warm water

¼ cup fish sauce

¼ cup distilled white vinegar

¼ cup sugar

2 garlic cloves, minced

Chili-garlic sauce (optional)

This is the traditional sauce served with Vietnamese noodle salads— it's the perfect mix of sweet, sour, salty, and spicy.

In a bowl, whisk together the water, fish sauce, vinegar, sugar, and garlic. If desired, add chili-garlic sauce to taste. Whisk until the sugar has dissolved. Serve immediately, or store in the refrigerator, covered, up to 1 week.

TAKE IT FROM ME Rice Noodle Tips

If you don't use rice noodles frequently, exploring the rice noodle section of a good Asian grocery store can be intimidating. Here's what you need to know:

• Rice noodles come in all sizes (often indicated by an S for small, M for medium, etc.), and they are available fresh and dried. While fresh noodles need to be refrigerated and used within the week, dried noodles are shelf-stable like wheat pasta.

• Always stir the noodles as soon as they start cooking, as well as once or twice during cooking, to prevent them from sticking to each other.

• Most packages have a cooking time printed on the back. Follow the package directions, but if there's a range, lean toward the shorter end of the cooking time—you want the noodles to still have a little bit of a bite, and if you cook them too long, they'll get gummy.

• Unlike wheat pasta, rice noodles always need to be rinsed with cool water after cooking. This removes the sticky starch that comes out of the noodles during the cooking process.

KIMCHI MAC AND CHEESE

SERVES 6 to 8   **TIME** 30 minutes, plus baking time

1 pound elbow macaroni

1 cup panko bread crumbs

1 tablespoon extra-virgin olive oil

4 tablespoons (½ stick) unsalted butter

2 tablespoons all-purpose flour

2 cups whole milk, warmed

1 tablespoon Dijon mustard

2 teaspoons gochujang

¼ teaspoon ground (or freshly grated) nutmeg

2 teaspoons kosher salt

2 cups grated Gruyère cheese

4 cups grated sharp cheddar cheese (such as Tillamook)

1 cup packed kimchi, roughly chopped

My ultimate homemade indulgence is an ooey, gooey, thick mac and cheese with a classic Honeysuckle twist: kimchi. The unexpected combination of sharp cheddar with the kimchi's spicy tang packs an incredible punch and is a guaranteed crowd-pleaser. I also kick up the spice level with a dab of gochujang. Serve this kimchi mac with my Pan-Seared Steak with Ssamjang Glaze (page 135) for an epic fusion feast.

1 Preheat the oven to 375°F.

2 Bring a pot of lightly salted water to a rapid boil. Add the macaroni and boil for 4 minutes. Drain, rinse with cold water, and set aside.

3 Meanwhile, put the panko in a bowl, drizzle with the olive oil, and mix until all the panko is evenly moist. Set aside.

4 In a heavy-bottomed ovenproof pot or Dutch oven, melt the butter over medium-low heat. Add the flour and whisk for 1 minute as the mixture bubbles. Drizzle in the warm milk, whisking to get rid of any clumps. Once the mixture is smooth, whisk in the mustard, gochujang, nutmeg, and salt. Switch to a wooden spoon and continue stirring until the sauce coats the back of the spoon. It'll just take a few minutes. (When you draw your finger across the back of the spoon, the sauce should be thick enough not to run into the line your finger makes.)

5 Remove from the heat and add both grated cheeses, the macaroni, and kimchi and mix until the pasta is completely coated with cheese and kimchi sauce. You can bake the mac and cheese right in the pot, as long as it's ovenproof, or you can pour the pasta into a wide, shallow casserole-style dish. Top with the panko mixture and transfer the pot or dish to the oven.

6 Bake for 15 to 20 minutes for a shallow casserole pan or 35 to 40 minutes if using a deeper pan, until the panko topping is golden brown and the cheese sauce is bubbling at the edges. The finished dish can be refrigerated for up to 3 days and reheated.

TAKE IT FROM ME The Four-Minute Miracle

Baking mac and cheese can be tricky—you want to cook the noodles first, but if you cook them too long, they get too soft after baking. I've found that 4 minutes is the perfect amount of time to cook the noodles before stirring them into the cheese sauce.

CHICKEN KATSU *with* MACARONI SALAD

SERVES 4   **TIME** 1 hour 15 minutes

FOR THE MACARONI SALAD

8 ounces (about 2 cups) elbow macaroni

½ cup plain Greek yogurt

¼ cup mayonnaise (preferably Kewpie)

1 tablespoon sugar

2 teaspoons cider vinegar

2 teaspoons kosher salt

2 stalks celery, finely diced

¼ yellow onion, finely minced

1 carrot

FOR THE CHICKEN KATSU

1 pound boneless, skinless chicken thighs

Kosher salt and freshly ground black pepper

½ cup all-purpose flour

2 large eggs, whisked to blend

1½ cups panko bread crumbs

Avocado oil (or other high smoke point oil), for frying, plus more as needed

Katsu Sauce (recipe follows), for serving

My earliest family vacation memories take place in Hawaii. We would go almost every year, and now it feels like another home. While my parents enjoyed the local fruits, many of which they had in Vietnam (which has a similar climate), I was out playing in the water or bumming on the sand. I still continue this tradition, but now with my own family. (I'm currently trying to convince Nate to move to the islands at least for six months of the year. Wish me luck.) Check out our last family trip to Oahu in my food tour vlog on *Honeysuckle*!

The vibe, at least in Honolulu, is completely different now than it was when I was growing up. For example, the International Marketplace, currently a high-end shopping mall with luxury stores lining the streets nearby, used to be nothing more than a casual food court, with something for everyone. They had Vietnamese food for my parents, while my sister and I explored all the local eats—poke, *kālua* pork, mac salad, loco moco, and other Hawaiian plate lunches. I couldn't choose which beloved favorite of mine to re-create for this book, so Erisy cast the deciding vote by actually eating my chicken katsu. Crusted in panko crumbs with a cold mac salad, this meal restores that aloha spirit wherever I might be.

There's not much hands-on time for this recipe—you just need to wait for the macaroni to cook and cool, so start that first, or even make the mac salad a day ahead and refrigerate it until you're ready to eat.

1 **MAKE THE MACARONI SALAD:** In a large pot of salted boiling water, cook the elbow macaroni until al dente, 8 to 10 minutes. Drain and rinse with cold water. Set aside to cool and drain for a few minutes.

2 Meanwhile, in a large bowl, whisk together the yogurt, mayonnaise, sugar, vinegar, and salt until smooth. Add the celery and onion. Grate the carrot on the small holes of a box grater, add it to the mixture, and stir to blend.

3 When the macaroni is ready, stir it in. (You can add a few tablespoons milk if or more mayonnaise if you'd like a saucier mac salad.) Cover and refrigerate for at least 1 hour (or up to 3 days) to let the flavors blend.

4 **MAKE THE CHICKEN KATSU:** Arrange the chicken thighs as flat as possible on a large cutting board and cover with plastic wrap. Using a meat pounder or the bottom of a small skillet, pound the chicken thighs to an even ½-inch thickness. Remove the plastic and season the chicken on both sides with salt and pepper.

5 SET UP A DREDGING STATION: In a wide, shallow bowl, combine the flour, 1 teaspoon salt, and pepper to taste. Place the whisked eggs a second bowl and the panko in a third bowl. Working with one piece of chicken at a time, dip the chicken first in the flour mixture, then in the egg, and finally in the panko, taking care to cover every part of the meat at each step. Transfer the coated chicken pieces to a plate and set aside.

6 Pour ¼ inch of oil into a large cast-iron skillet. Set over medium-high heat and let the oil get good and hot, about 350°F. (You can test this by throwing in a small piece of panko. If it sizzles vigorously, the oil is ready!) Add 2 pieces of chicken to the pan and fry until the chicken is golden brown on both sides and cooked through, 3 to 5 minutes on each side, depending on the thickness of your chicken. Transfer the chicken to a plate lined with paper towels. Repeat with the remaining chicken, adding a bit more oil to the pan, if needed, so the oil coats the bottom of the pan before you add the next batch.

7 Cut the chicken into 1-inch strips and serve hot, with the katsu sauce for dipping and the mac salad.

KATSU SAUCE

MAKES about ¾ cup   **TIME** 5 minutes

½ cup ketchup

2 tablespoons Worcestershire sauce

2 tablespoon soy sauce

1 teaspoon Dijon mustard

½ teaspoon garlic powder

In a small bowl, stir together the ketchup, Worcestershire sauce, soy sauce, mustard, and garlic powder.

Store any leftover sauce in the refrigerator, covered, for up to a week.

MISO UDON CARBONARA

SERVES 2 to 4   **TIME** 20 minutes

3 large eggs

2 tablespoons heavy cream

1 tablespoon red or yellow miso

½ cup grated Parmesan cheese

1 teaspoon coarsely ground black pepper

1 tablespoon unsalted butter

4 slices bacon, chopped into ¾-inch pieces

1 garlic clove, minced

1 pound fresh Sanuki-style udon noodles

3 scallions (green parts only), slivered

Shichimi togarashi (Japanese chile powder blend)

Silky, creamy, pasta carbonara is a revelation every time it's eaten. Made with only a few simple ingredients—eggs, bacon, and good Parmesan cheese—it's an experience beyond pleasure and proof that eggs are magical. Here's the Honeysuckle twist: Use fresh, springy udon noodles instead of pasta (I like the square-edged Sanuki style of udon, which are chewier and have a nice silky mouthfeel) and a dash of miso for extra umami.

This is a dish, however, that requires some technique. The sauce is delicate since it begins with raw eggs that need to be slowly incorporated and cooked with the heat from the noodles and bacon, without scrambling them. Have the scallions and serving dish ready before cooking so they can be used immediately after the sauce is done.

Can't find fresh udon noodles at your local store? Simply use frozen or dried noodles, cooked according to the package directions, before mixing them in with the bacon.

1 Bring a large pot of salted water (at least 7 cups) to a boil.

2 Meanwhile, in a bowl, whisk together the eggs, cream, miso, Parmesan, and black pepper. Set aside.

3 In a large skillet, melt the butter over medium-high heat. Add the bacon and cook, stirring occasionally, until golden brown, about 5 minutes. Add the garlic and cook for another minute, stirring frequently. Remove the pan from the heat and set aside to cool slightly.

4 Add the udon to the boiling water and cook according to package directions (usually about 4 minutes for al dente noodles). Scoop the hot noodles directly into the skillet with the bacon, reserving the noodle cooking water.

5 Drizzle the egg mixture over the noodles, stirring as you add it, until the egg mixture coats all the noodles. You don't want the eggs to scramble against the pan, so mix constantly until you get a nice, smooth, creamy sauce. If you want the sauce to be a little looser, add 2 tablespoons at a time of the reserved noodle cooking water until you get the consistency you want. If you prefer a thicker sauce, turn the heat back on low and let the sauce thicken while stirring the noodles constantly.

6 Serve immediately, garnished with a sprinkle of scallions and shichimi togarashi.

BAKED RIGATONI *with* SAUSAGE AND EGGPLANT

SERVES 4 TIME 1 hour

3 cups (about 8 ounces) rigatoni pasta

4 tablespoons extra-virgin olive oil

½ medium eggplant, cut into 1-inch cubes (about 2 cups)

½ small onion, finely chopped

½ pound spicy or sweet Italian sausage (casings removed, if applicable)

3 garlic cloves, finely chopped

1 (28-ounce) can crushed tomatoes

1 teaspoon dried oregano

1 teaspoon Italian seasoning (or a mixture of dried basil, thyme, rosemary, oregano, and/or marjoram)

1 tablespoon julienned fresh basil, plus more for garnish

1 teaspoon kosher salt

2 tablespoons grated Parmesan cheese

¼ cup heavy cream

½ cup shredded mozzarella cheese

Looking for a simple weeknight meal? This cheesy baked rigatoni is at the top of my list. I add eggplant to amp up the nutrition, but it's still one of those dinners where the table gets very quiet, because each person is completely enjoying their dinner. And it's even more intense the next day, after the flavors have completely soaked into the softened pasta. Make this a day ahead and reheat before serving. You can also double the recipe and bake it in a 9 × 13-inch baking dish.

You can use firm packaged mozzarella or fresh mozzarella here, or even the preshredded kind, for convenience. They'll all be delicious!

1 Preheat the oven to 375°F.

2 In a large pot of salted boiling water, cook the rigatoni for 8 minutes exactly. (It won't be cooked through, but it will finish cooking in the oven later. Trust me!) Drain and set aside.

3 In a well-seasoned 10-inch cast-iron or nonstick skillet, heat 3 tablespoons of the olive oil over medium heat. Add the eggplant, stir to coat all the pieces in oil, and cook, stirring and turning occasionally, until soft and golden brown on all sides, about 10 minutes. (The eggplant will soak up the olive oil as it cooks.) Transfer the eggplant to a bowl and set side.

4 In the same skillet, heat the remaining 1 tablespoon oil. Add the onion and cook, stirring, until fragrant, about 3 minutes. Add the sausage, breaking it into bite-size pieces as you add it to the pan. Cook, breaking up the sausage with a wooden spoon a little bit more as

it cooks, until browned and cooked through, 7 to 8 minutes. Add the garlic, crushed tomatoes, dried oregano, Italian seasoning, fresh basil, salt, Parmesan, and heavy cream. Stir until the sauce becomes thoroughly pink. Add the cooked rigatoni and reserved eggplant to the sauce and mix again until each piece of pasta is covered in sauce.

5 Transfer the mixture to an 8 × 8-inch baking pan and sprinkle with the shredded mozzarella. (If you've prepared the pasta in a cast-iron skillet, you can also just bake it right in the skillet.) Bake for 18 to 20 minutes, until the sauce is bubbling and the cheese is golden brown. Garnish with chopped basil and serve hot, or let the dish cool completely, then wrap well in plastic and refrigerate or freeze. To reheat the rigatoni (thawed overnight in the fridge if it was frozen), remove the plastic and reheat for 15 minutes in a preheated 350°F oven.

SESAME SOBA NOODLE STIR-FRY

SERVES 4 **TIME** 20 minutes

⅓ cup soy sauce

3 tablespoons sesame oil

1 tablespoon plus 1 teaspoon
extra-virgin olive oil

1 tablespoon tahini or smooth
peanut butter

1 tablespoon honey

4 garlic cloves, minced

1 teaspoon grated peeled
fresh ginger

1 teaspoon rice vinegar

1 teaspoon kosher salt

1 tablespoon chili-garlic sauce,
or to taste (optional)

1 (9.5-ounce) package
dried soba noodles (such as
Hakubaku brand)

1 tablespoon neutral-tasting oil
(such as avocado oil)

2 stalks celery, thinly sliced
(about 1 cup)

1 cup thick-sliced napa cabbage

1 carrot, shredded

1 cup snow peas

I have a lot of soba noodle stir-fries on my channel, mostly because they adapt well to so many different flavors. This one combines a hefty amount of fresh veggies with homemade sesame noodles and can be quite satiating just like this. Or if you want a more substantial meal, make it a sidekick to some Honey-Soy Glazed Ribs (page 169), Grilled Salmon with Tamarind Dipping Sauce (page 132), or Pan-Seared Steak with Ssamjang Glaze (page 135).

1 Bring a large pot of water to a boil over high heat.

2 Meanwhile, in a bowl, whisk together the soy sauce, sesame oil, 1 tablespoon of the olive oil, the tahini, honey, half the garlic, the ginger, rice vinegar, and salt. If desired, add chili-garlic sauce to taste. Don't worry if the sauce appears to be clumpy; the noodles will take care of that later.

3 When the water boils, drizzle in the remaining 1 teaspoon olive oil, then add the soba noodles. Cook the noodles for 1 minute less than the package directions (about 3 minutes), then drain well and rinse with warm water.

4 In a wok, heat the neutral oil over high heat. When the oil begins to smoke, add the celery, cabbage, carrot, snow peas, and remaining garlic and cook, stirring constantly until the vegetables begin to soften, about 2 minutes. Add the noodles to the wok and add the sauce. Remove the pan from the heat, stir until the sauce coats all the noodles and vegetables, and serve.

RAINBOW GRAIN BOWLS

SERVES 4 TIME 1 hour

FOR THE TAHINI SAUCE

¼ cup tahini

¼ cup warm water, plus more as needed

2 tablespoons lemon juice

1 tablespoon extra-virgin olive oil

1 teaspoon kosher salt

1 teaspoon honey

½ teaspoon garlic powder

½ teaspoon ground cumin

FOR THE GRAIN BOWLS

5 tablespoons plus 2 teaspoons extra-virgin olive oil

1 teaspoon garlic powder

1 teaspoon ground turmeric

2 heaping cups cauliflower florets (from ½ small head), cut into bite-size pieces

3 carrots, cut into 2-inch lengths and quartered

Kosher salt and freshly ground black pepper

½ cup quinoa, rinsed

4 cups chopped kale (any kind)

2 cups packed mixed greens

1 pint cherry or grape tomatoes, halved

1 large avocado, quartered and sliced lengthwise

½ cup Quick Pickled Red Onions (page 198)

½ cup crumbled feta cheese

½ cup toasted pumpkin seeds

Grain bowls are more of an ingredient-rich compilation than an actual recipe. For me, they tend to be a mix of whatever looks good in my fridge, and I encourage you to get inspiration from what's already on hand! But it gets really fun when the bowls are colorful and have playful textures. My rainbow bowl (or shall we say "rain-bowl"?) highlights every bold color and makes for a filling lunch or dinner. It can even be prepped ahead of time in mason jars to last the whole week. (I used quinoa here but this can be done with farro, bulgur, brown rice, or any grain of choice.)

1 MAKE THE TAHINI SAUCE: In a small bowl, whisk together the tahini, warm water, lemon juice, olive oil, salt, honey, garlic powder, and cumin until smooth. If you want the sauce to be thicker, leave it as is (it will thicken as it stands); otherwise, whisk in additional warm water, up to ¼ cup, until the sauce is the consistency you like. (The sauce can be stored in the refrigerator, covered, for up to 1 week.)

2 Preheat the oven to 450°F. Line a rimmed baking sheet with foil and put it in the oven to preheat. Let the baking sheet heat in the oven for 10 minutes after the oven comes to temperature.

3 PREPARE THE GRAIN BOWLS: In a large bowl, stir together 3 tablespoons of the olive oil, the garlic powder, and turmeric. Add the cauliflower and carrots and toss until the vegetables are completely coated, then season to taste with salt and pepper. Transfer the vegetables to the preheated baking sheet and bake for 18 to 20 minutes, until the cauliflower is golden brown and the carrots are soft, turning and shaking the pan about halfway through.

4 In a heavy-bottomed pot with a lid, heat 2 teaspoons of the olive oil over medium-high heat. Add the quinoa and let it toast for about 3 minutes, stirring frequently. Pour in 1 cup water and bring the mixture to a boil. Once the liquid has absorbed, reduce the heat to the lowest setting and cover the pot. Let the quinoa cook until the liquid has been completely absorbed, another 5 to 7 minutes. Remove the pan from the heat and fluff the quinoa with a fork. Set aside.

5 In a large skillet, heat the remaining 2 tablespoons olive oil over medium heat. Add the kale, season with salt, and cook, stirring, until the kale is wilted, about 5 minutes. Transfer to a plate and set aside.

6 To assemble the grain bowls, divide the mixed greens among four bowls. Then dividing evenly, spoon the quinoa over the salad. Arrange the kale, tomatoes, avocado, pickled onions, feta, and pumpkin seeds on top of the quinoa. Add the roasted carrots and cauliflower. Drizzle with the tahini sauce and enjoy!

ROCKIN' BEEF BOWL

SERVES 4 to 6   **TIME** 30 minutes, plus marinating time

FOR THE BEEF

2 tablespoons oyster sauce

2 garlic cloves, minced

1 teaspoon sugar

1 teaspoon soy sauce

1 teaspoon fish sauce

¼ teaspoon sesame oil

1½ pounds tri-tip steak, cut into 1-inch cubes

2 tablespoons neutral-tasting oil (such as avocado oil)

FOR THE WATERCRESS SALAD

2 tablespoons rice vinegar

1 teaspoon sugar

1 teaspoon neutral-tasting oil (such as avocado oil)

½ teaspoon salt

Freshly ground black pepper

1 red onion, thinly sliced

1 bunch watercress or upland cress (about 3 ounces greens)

FOR SERVING

Tomato-Fried Rice (page 193)

1 tomato, quartered

Pickled Carrots and Daikon (page 198)

My parents taught me how to cook Shaking Beef (*bò lúc lac*) when I was very young. It's a classic Vietnamese sizzling beef stir-fry served with a tomato-fried rice and a sharp watercress salad. When Nate first tried my version of this he looked at me and said, "This rocks!" The name just stuck, and that's what we call it. I prefer a tri-tip cut for the steak, but beef tenderloin, sirloin, or rib-eye work just as well—and the longer you marinate the beef, the more flavor it will have. Also, day-old rice is perfect for the tomato-fried rice.

1 **MARINATE THE BEEF:** In a large bowl, stir together the oyster sauce, garlic, sugar, soy sauce, fish sauce, and sesame oil to blend. Add the meat, stir to coat all the pieces evenly, and marinate for 30 minutes at room temperature or in the fridge, covered, for 2 hours (or overnight).

2 **MAKE THE WATERCRESS SALAD:** In a bowl, whisk together the rice vinegar, 2 tablespoons water, the sugar, neutral oil, salt, and black pepper to taste. Toss with the sliced onion and watercress. Set aside.

3 When ready to serve, make the tomato-fried rice as directed and transfer it to a platter.

4 **TO COOK THE BEEF:** In a large skillet or wok heat the neutral oil over high heat. Add about half the beef and cook, turning occasionally, until the beef is well browned on all sides, 2 or 3 minutes total. Transfer the meat to the platter with the rice, then repeat with the remaining meat. (Go ahead and add those yummy juices from the pan to the rice at the end.)

5 Pile the watercress salad directly on top of the beef and rice—the watercress will steam and soften a bit. Garnish with the tomato quarters and pickled carrots and daikon and serve immediately.

THAI SHRIMP-FRIED RICE

SERVES 4   **TIME** 30 minutes

FOR THE SAUCE

1 tablespoon fish sauce

1 tablespoon soy sauce

1 tablespoon Thai red curry paste (such as Thai Kitchen brand)

1 teaspoon sugar

½ teaspoon kosher salt

Juice of ½ lime

FOR THE FRIED RICE

2 tablespoons neutral-tasting oil (such as avocado oil)

¼ pound green beans, trimmed and chopped into pea-size pieces (about 1 cup chopped)

½ red bell pepper, halved lengthwise and sliced ¼ inch wide

¼ yellow onion, halved and cut into ¼-inch-thick slices

3 garlic cloves, minced

¼ teaspoon grated peeled fresh ginger

¾ pound large shrimp (about 12), peeled and deveined, tail left intact

½ teaspoon kosher salt

2 large eggs, whisked to blend

4 cups cold cooked White Rice (page 192)

1 tomato, cut into wedges

½ cucumber, cut into rounds

1 lime, cut into wedges

4 sprigs fresh cilantro

Thai Town in Los Angeles is the largest Thai community outside of Thailand. I am thrilled to have moved so close to Thai Town, and we've been hungrily exploring this neighborhood since coming to LA. Thai Town has opened my eyes to a whole world beyond the usual pad Thais and curries. At Jitlada (a now-famous family-owned spot), I was so inspired by their spicy fried rice that I had to try to re-create something similar myself.

1 **MAKE THE SAUCE:** In a small bowl, whisk together the fish sauce, soy sauce, curry paste, sugar, salt, and lime juice until blended. Set aside.

2 **MAKE THE FRIED RICE:** Heat a large wok over high heat, then add 1 tablespoon of the oil. Add the green beans and red bell pepper and sauté until the pepper loses its brightness, a minute or two. Add the onion, garlic, and ginger and continue to stir-fry until fragrant, another 1 to 2 minutes. Add the shrimp and salt and keep everything moving until the shrimp is pink and cooked on all sides, 2 to 3 minutes more. Transfer the shrimp mixture to a bowl.

3 Add the remaining 1 tablespoon oil to the hot wok. Add the eggs and let them settle against the bottom of the pan. Quickly break up the eggs with your cooking spoon and add the cold rice. Break up the rice and mix it with the eggs.

4 Add the sauce and continue mixing until the rice warms up and the grains separate. Return the shrimp mixture to the wok and cook, stirring, for another few minutes to heat everything through. Transfer the rice to plates. Garnish the rice with tomato wedges, sliced cucumbers, a wedge of lime, and a few sprigs of cilantro. Enjoy! (This is best eaten the same day.)

CHICKEN TINGA BURRITO BOWL

SERVES 4   **TIME** 1 hour

FOR THE CHICKEN TINGA

1 (14.5-ounce) can fire-roasted diced tomatoes

1 canned chipotle pepper in adobo sauce, plus 1 tablespoon adobo sauce

½ cup low-sodium chicken broth

½ yellow onion, chopped

3 garlic cloves, smashed and peeled

1 teaspoon dried Mexican oregano

1 teaspoon ground cumin

1 teaspoon kosher salt

1 tablespoon extra-virgin olive oil

2 pounds boneless, skinless chicken thighs

FOR SERVING

2 cups cooked brown or white rice (see Flawlessly Cooked Rice, page 192)

4 cups shredded green leaf or romaine lettuce (from half an 8-ounce head)

1 (15-ounce) can black beans, rinsed and drained, warmed

1 pint cherry tomatoes, halved (or quartered if large)

2 avocados, sliced

½ cup crumbled queso fresco

¼ cup roughly chopped fresh cilantro

Quick Chipotle Salsa (page 60) or store-bought salsa, for serving

1 lime, cut into wedges

It's not surprising that I'm often asked for chicken recipes on my channel—my viewers use chicken so frequently as a main ingredient that they often need new meal inspiration. This Mexican-style shredded chicken, served in a fiery chipotle tomato stew, has become one of our family's go-to chicken recipes.

1 PREPARE THE CHICKEN TINGA: In a blender, whirl together the fire-roasted tomatoes, chipotle pepper, adobo sauce, broth, onion, garlic, oregano, cumin, and salt until smooth.

2 Heat a large, heavy-bottomed soup pot or Dutch oven over medium-high heat. Add the olive oil, then add the tomato mixture and bring to a simmer. Nestle the chicken thighs into the sauce, turn to coat, cover, and simmer over medium-low heat. Stir occasionally until the chicken is tender enough to pull apart with a fork, 30 to 40 minutes. Remove from the heat and use two large forks to shred the chicken. (Here, the chicken tinga can be cooled, then refrigerated for up to 3 days and reheated before serving.)

3 When ready to serve, divide the rice, lettuce, beans, tomatoes, and avocados among four bowls. Scoop some of the chicken tinga onto the bowl with some sauce and top with a sprinkle of queso fresco and chopped cilantro, plus salsa to taste and a squeeze of lime. Enjoy!

TAKE IT FROM ME Breast or Thigh?

Chicken breast can be used but it tends to be a bit dry. I prefer to use chicken thigh as it has more flavor.

give me an hour
WEEKNIGHT MAINS

When I'm short on time but feeling inspired to really cook up a storm, I turn to the following recipes. They are some of my most creative entrées, pushing the boundaries of typical weeknight fare—but they are all ready within an hour.

LEMONGRASS CHICKEN STIR-FRY (GÀ XÀO SẢ ỚT)

SERVES 4 **TIME** 45 minutes

4 tablespoons grated or finely minced lemongrass

3 garlic cloves, minced

2 tablespoons fish sauce

1 teaspoon Madras curry powder

1 teaspoon ground turmeric

1 teaspoon sugar

½ teaspoon minced fresh ginger

½ teaspoon kosher salt

¼ teaspoon red pepper flakes (optional)

2 pounds boneless, skinless chicken thighs, cut into 1 × 2-inch pieces

1 tablespoon neutral-tasting oil (such as avocado oil)

½ white onion, diced

The flavor profile of this sautéed chicken recipe is found in many different Vietnamese dishes. The meat is marinated in a lemongrass mixture with a kick of curry powder (my mom's trick) to heighten the lemongrass essence. You can also grill the meat instead of stir-frying it; try using this version as a substitute for the pork for the Vietnamese Grilled Pork Noodle Salad (page 110).

1 In a large bowl, combine 2 tablespoons of the lemongrass, the garlic, fish sauce, curry powder, turmeric, sugar, ginger, salt, and red pepper flakes, if using. Add the chicken and mix to coat every piece. Set the chicken aside to marinate for about 20 minutes.

2 Heat a large cast-iron skillet or wok over medium-high heat. When hot, add the oil, onion, and the remaining 2 tablespoons lemongrass and stir-fry until fragrant, 2 to 3 minutes. Add the chicken and cook, stirring constantly to keep the chicken moving so it doesn't burn, until the chicken is cooked through and golden brown, 7 to 9 minutes. Serve with rice.

GRILLED SALMON *with* TAMARIND DIPPING SAUCE

SERVES 4 to 6   **TIME** 30 minutes

FOR THE TAMARIND DIPPING SAUCE

1 tablespoon avocado oil

2 garlic cloves, minced

½ cup tamarind paste, store-bought or homemade (see page 97)

2 tablespoons dark brown sugar

2 tablespoons fish sauce

Juice of ½ lime

1 fresh red Thai chile, finely chopped (optional)

FOR THE SALMON

1 (2-pound) skin-on salmon fillet (about ¾ inch thick at thickest point)

2 tablespoons avocado oil, plus more for the grill grates

Kosher salt and freshly ground black pepper

½ cup Scallion Relish (page 201)

⅓ cup Fried Shallots (page 201)

3 tablespoons chopped peanuts

I often talk about my mom and grandma cooking at home, but my dad certainly enjoyed cooking our meals also. Until recently I remembered this grilled salmon dinner as his handiwork, but my mom gently corrected me and took credit for this recipe. I think if he were still with us, there might be some disagreement, so I'll just say it's from both of them. I can so clearly recall eating it: The salmon was tucked into tidy spring rolls with fresh herbs (like in Choose Your Own Adventure: Spring Rolls, page 181) and we'd all sit together and chat as they were being prepared. Nowadays I make the salmon for Erisy because fish is her favorite food! We'll enjoy it along with a side of my Crispy Brussels Sprouts with Chile-Lime-Garlic Sauce (page 191), brown rice, and extra scoops of the tangy tamarind sauce.

1 **MAKE THE TAMARIND DIPPING SAUCE:** In a medium saucepan, heat the oil over medium heat until shimmering. Reduce the heat to the lowest setting, add the garlic, and cook until it turns a light golden brown, about 1 minute. Add the tamarind paste, brown sugar, and fish sauce. Adjust the heat to a simmer and cook for about 5 minutes to thicken a bit, then add the lime juice. Remove from the heat and transfer to a bowl. If using the chile, stir it in and let the sauce cool completely before serving.

2 **COOK THE SALMON:** Heat a gas or charcoal grill to medium heat (about 400°F). Brush the cooking grates clean. Brush the salmon on both sides with the oil, then season the flesh side with salt and pepper.

Brush or rub the grates with oil, then place the salmon over direct heat, skin-side up, cover, and grill until the fish releases easily from the grill, about 4 minutes. Turn the fish and repeat on the second side, grilling until the fish is opaque at the edges but still a bit shiny in the center, another 4 minutes (or a few minutes longer for a thicker cut of fish). (If you don't have a grill, you could always cook in a cast-iron skillet over medium-high heat for 4 minutes on each side for a perfect medium, or more for thicker cuts.)

3 Transfer the fish to a plate, then spread the scallion relish on top and sprinkle with fried shallots and chopped peanuts. Serve with the sauce for dipping or drizzling. (This is best eaten the same day.)

PAN-SEARED STEAK *with* SSAMJANG GLAZE

SERVES 2 to 4   **TIME** 25 minutes

FOR THE STEAKS

2 (12-ounce) steaks (top sirloin, rib-eye, or New York strip), each 1¼ to 1½ inches thick

Kosher salt

4 tablespoons neutral-tasting oil (such as avocado oil)

2 garlic cloves, smashed with the peel on

1 tablespoon unsalted butter

FOR THE GLAZE

2 tablespoons ssamjang

1 tablespoon soy sauce

1 tablespoon sesame oil

¼ teaspoon sugar

Toasted sesame seeds, for garnish

2 scallions, chopped, for garnish

LA is a huge, busy city—the traffic is so bad that it can take well over an hour to travel just a few short miles—and I often tell Nate we can't ever move too far from where we live now because it would take us too long to get to Koreatown. I'm so appreciative that we're close to the concentration of Korean culture surrounding the intersection of Western Avenue and Olympic Boulevard. There's karaoke, late-night bar crawls, Korean barbecue ("KBBQ"), and a mix of coffee, dumplings, local eats, and Asian grocery markets all within a few blocks. This pan-seared steak is my homage to all the best memories I've experienced so far in LA's Koreatown. The *ssamjang* glaze represents the colors of hot nights after a smoky KBBQ smackdown, and the sesame oil dipping sauce for the *ssam* lettuce wrap packs a knockout flavor.

---

1 COOK THE STEAKS: Remove the steaks from the refrigerator and let them sit for about 30 minutes at room temperature. Pat the steaks dry with a paper towel, then generously sprinkle each steak on both sides with salt.

2 Heat a large cast-iron pan over high heat. Add 2 tablespoons of the neutral oil and when it begins to smoke, add one steak and cook, undisturbed, for 3 to 4 minutes (for medium-rare) or 4 to 5 minutes (for medium), depending on the steak's thickness. Turn the steak and cook for another 2 minutes, then add one of the garlic cloves and half of the butter. Carefully tilt the pan away from you and, using a spoon, scoop up some of the garlic butter and pour it all over the steak, repeating until the steak

is shiny, about 30 seconds. Let the steak cook another 2 to 3 minutes, then transfer it to a plate to rest for at least 5 minutes. Carefully wipe the pan out and repeat with the remaining oil, steak, garlic, and butter.

3 WHILE THE STEAKS REST, MAKE THE GLAZE: In a bowl, whisk together the *ssamjang*, soy sauce, 1 tablespoon water, the sesame oil, and sugar until blended.

4 Slice the steaks across the grain into 1-inch-thick strips, then drizzle as much or as little of the *ssamjang* glaze over the steak as you'd like, garnish with sesame seeds and scallions, and serve immediately, with the remaining glaze alongside for dipping.

Note It's important to cook the steaks one at a time, because if you crowd the pan, you risk steaming the meat instead of searing it. Also, make sure you have your stove's ventilation fan on, or open a window. These steaks are smokin' hot!

ORANGE CAULIFLOWER NUGGETS

SERVES 4   **TIME** 1 hour

As I mentioned, cauliflower is having a major moment, especially as a satisfying substitute for meat. If you're feeling that you need to go meatless, try these tangy orange chicken "nuggets," a throwback to our nostalgic takeout memories. Cauliflower is exceptional with its meaty texture and versatility. So enjoy these zesty bites with a side of brown rice and stir-fried veggies for a filling midweek dinner.

FOR THE GLAZE

1 tablespoon extra-virgin olive oil

1 teaspoon grated peeled fresh ginger

3 garlic cloves, minced

1 tablespoon grated orange zest

1 cup fresh orange juice

¼ cup soy sauce

¼ cup rice vinegar

3 tablespoons dark brown sugar

1 tablespoon oyster sauce

1 tablespoon cornstarch

FOR THE CAULIFLOWER

1 cup all-purpose flour

1 cup whole milk

1 teaspoon kosher salt

¼ teaspoon freshly ground black pepper

1 medium head cauliflower (about 2½ pounds), cut into large bite-size florets, rinsed, and dried

3 cups panko bread crumbs

1 Preheat the oven to 400°F. Line a rimmed baking sheet with foil.

2 **MAKE THE GLAZE:** In a saucepan, heat the olive oil over medium heat. When hot, add the ginger and garlic and cook until fragrant, about 1 minute. Add the orange zest, orange juice, soy sauce, rice vinegar, brown sugar, and oyster sauce. Stir to dissolve the sugar and let the sauce come to a simmer. Cook for 3 minutes, stirring occasionally. Meanwhile, in a small bowl, whisk together the cornstarch and ¼ cup water until smooth. Pour the mixture into the sauce and whisk until the sauce boils and thickens. Remove from the heat and set the glaze aside to cool.

3 **PREPARE THE CAULIFLOWER:** In a large bowl, whisk together the flour, milk, salt, and pepper until it forms a smooth, thick batter. Add the cauliflower florets and stir to make sure each one is coated with the batter. (I like to use my hands for this, so each floret gets coated evenly.)

4 Put the panko in a separate bowl. Working with a few florets at a time, dip each coated floret into the panko, allowing any excess batter to drip off as you remove them from the bowl, then rolling and turning them to make sure they're completely covered in crumbs. Transfer to the prepared baking sheet and repeat with the remaining cauliflower.

5 Bake the coated cauliflower for 12 minutes, or until just beginning to brown at the edges. Transfer to a large bowl. (Leave the oven on.)

6 Carefully place an ovenproof wire rack over the foil on the baking sheet. Drizzle the glaze over the cauliflower in the bowl, stir gently to coat all the florets evenly in the glaze. Transfer the glazed florets to the wire rack, allowing any extra glaze to drip back into the bowl first.

7 Return the coated cauliflower to the oven and bake for another 10 minutes, or until the coating crisps back up a bit and the cauliflower is tender all the way through. Serve immediately.

SALT AND PEPPER SHRIMP (TOM RANG MUOI)

SERVES 2 to 4   **TIME** 30 minutes

1 pound medium (21/25) tiger shrimp, unpeeled but deveined

½ cup cornstarch

Kosher salt and freshly ground black pepper

1 teaspoon garlic powder

Neutral-tasting oil (such as avocado oil)

3 garlic cloves

1 shallot, finely chopped

1 scallion (green part only), chopped

1 fresh red Thai chile, sliced (optional)

1 tablespoon chopped fresh cilantro, for garnish

Whenever my family was invited to a beautiful, lavish Chinese wedding (which seemed awfully frequent when I was a kid), my sister, Tram, and I would secretly look forward to the grand banquet following the ceremony. My favorite part was the peppery shellfish. I always considered this salt and pepper shrimp a dish reserved for special celebrations until I decided to make it part of the weeknight rotation. *Tom rang muoi* literally translates to "shrimp seasoned with salt and pepper." It's pan-fried to a crisp with the shells intact, which add a buttery crunch. (The shells are completely edible.) Although it's more authentic in Vietnamese cuisine to leave the shells on, you can certainly peel the shrimp if you prefer. Just leave the tails intact and coat them with the cornstarch mixture just before frying. Frozen shrimp work well also, but make sure they're completely thawed so they don't release extra water during the frying process.

Serve with rice (see page 192) and steamed vegetables, or on top of the Chile-Lime Street Fruit Salad (page 78) or the Sesame Soba Noodle Stir-Fry (page 121).

1 Fill a large bowl with ice, add water to cover, and then add the shrimp. This will help tighten the meat and make it nice and "crunchy" or firm. Soak the shrimp for 5 minutes.

2 In a medium bowl, stir together the cornstarch, 2 teaspoons salt, 1 teaspoon pepper, and the garlic powder. Set aside.

3 **MAKE THE SHALLOT MIXTURE:** Heat a large cast-iron skillet over medium heat. Drizzle in 1 tablespoon oil and toss in the garlic, shallot, scallion, and chile (if using). Cook and stir until fragrant, a minute or so, then transfer the mixture to a bowl and set aside.

4 Drain the shrimp and pat dry with paper towels, then add all the shrimp to the cornstarch mixture. Toss to coat each piece thoroughly.

5 Pour ¼ inch of oil into the same skillet and set over medium-high heat. When the oil is hot enough that any leftover shallots are sizzling vigorously, working in batches, add about 6 shrimp to the pan. Fry until golden brown, about 2 minutes, then flip to the other side. Cook the other side until golden brown, another minute. Transfer the shrimp to a plate lined with paper towels and give them another quick sprinkle of salt and pepper. Make sure to do this while the shrimp is still piping hot so that the salt and pepper sticks. Repeat until all the shrimp are cooked, adding more oil to the pan as necessary.

6 Garnish with the reserved shallot mixture, sprinkle with fresh cilantro, and serve piping hot. (This is best eaten immediately.) Enjoy!

SQUASH TACOS *with* CILANTRO-LIME SLAW

SERVES 4   TIME 40 minutes

FOR THE TACO FILLING

2 teaspoons chili powder

2 garlic cloves, minced

1 teaspoon ground cumin

1 teaspoon kosher salt

½ teaspoon paprika

2 tablespoons extra-virgin olive oil

1 pound peeled butternut squash, cut into ½-inch cubes (see Note)

1 (15-ounce) can black beans, rinsed and drained

FOR THE SLAW

3 tablespoons plain Greek yogurt

3 tablespoons lime juice

2 tablespoons chopped fresh cilantro

1 teaspoon kosher salt

1 teaspoon sugar

2 cups thinly sliced red cabbage

2 cups thinly sliced green cabbage

1 scallion (green part only), sliced

FOR THE TACOS

8 corn tortillas, warmed (see Heating Tortillas, page 59)

Quick Pickled Red Onions (page 198)

½ cup crumbled queso fresco

Cilantro sprigs, for serving

Lime wedges, for serving

Mexican crema, for drizzling

We left many dear friends behind when we moved out of the Bay Area. Yohann and Kacey were some of our closest friends, and we miss seeing them as often as we once did. As vegetarians they always exposed us to new takes on food that we quickly grew to love. When I made a complete taco bar spread (including my Pressure Cooker Carnitas, page 162) for our first baby's gender reveal party, I added a plate of these butternut squash and black bean tacos. I immediately knew this recipe was a hit—let's just say that more than two people enjoyed them! They're equally perfect as weeknight fare for your family and for wowing guests at an event. Here I add a tangy cilantro-lime slaw for added freshness and crunch.

It's best to make the pickled onions first, so they have time to sit before you eat. And yes, preheating the baking sheet for the squash is important—it gives them a good sear (see Get It Hot, page 191).

---

1 Preheat the oven to 400°F. Line a rimmed baking sheet with foil and put it in the oven to preheat. Let the pan heat in the oven for 10 minutes after the oven has come to temperature.

2 PREPARE THE TACO FILLING: In a bowl, whisk together the chili powder, garlic, cumin, salt, paprika, and olive oil. Add the squash and mix to coat all the pieces well. Remove the baking sheet from the oven and add the squash. Roast the squash for 12 to 15 minutes, until soft and beginning to brown, turning and shaking the pan about halfway through. Transfer the squash to a bowl and gently stir in the black beans.

3 MEANWHILE, MAKE THE SLAW: In a medium bowl, stir together the yogurt, lime juice, cilantro, salt, and sugar to blend. Add the red cabbage, green cabbage, and scallion, stir until all the vegetables are coated, season to taste, and set aside. (You can store the slaw in the refrigerator, covered, for up to 3 days before serving.)

4 ASSEMBLE THE TACOS (or let guests fill their own): Serve the tortillas with the squash and bean filling, the slaw, pickled onions, queso fresco, cilantro, limes, and *crema*.

Note I often buy a 1-pound package of precut butternut squash in the refrigerated produce section to make life easier.

CHICKEN ADOBO

SERVES 4 to 8   TIME 50 minutes

2 tablespoons coconut oil

4 bone-in, skin-on chicken thighs (about 1½ pounds total)

4 bone-in, skin-on chicken drumsticks (about 1½ pounds total)

Kosher salt and freshly ground black pepper

⅓ cup rice vinegar

½ cup soy sauce

½ cup full-fat canned coconut milk

6 garlic cloves, smashed and peeled

3 bay leaves

1 teaspoon black peppercorns

1 teaspoon sugar

Here's another chicken recipe that will hit the dinner jackpot. Chicken adobo is a classic Filipino bone-in chicken dish, simmered in a mixture of vinegar and soy sauce. When the recipe debuted on my channel, a viewer suggested I add a splash of coconut milk. I tried it, and it makes the sauce even better! I typically use both chicken thighs and legs and serve them with grilled eggplant and a mountain of rice to soak up all the stewy juices.

1 In a large Dutch oven or cast-iron skillet, melt the coconut oil over medium-high heat. Season the chicken on all sides with salt and pepper. When the oil is hot, add the chicken thighs and cook skin-side down until nicely browned, about 5 minutes. Transfer the chicken to a plate and repeat with the chicken drumsticks, cooking them for about 8 minutes, turning them when they release easily from the pan.

2 Add the vinegar, soy sauce, coconut milk, garlic, bay leaves, peppercorns, sugar, and ½ teaspoon salt to the pan, stir to blend, and return the chicken to the pan. Cover and cook the chicken over medium heat until cooked through, about 30 minutes, turning the chicken over about halfway through.

3 Serve as is, or transfer the chicken to a plate, increase the heat to medium-high, and simmer the sauce until it's thick enough to coat the back of a spoon, then drizzle it over the chicken. (The sauce will taste more concentrated this way, which is delicious, but it denies you the pleasure of having extra sauce—pick what you like best!) The finished adobo can be refrigerated for up to 3 days and reheated.

TRUFFLED MUSHROOM FLATBREAD PIZZA

MAKES 2 flatbread pizzas **TIME** 20 minutes

1 tablespoon unsalted butter

8 ounces cremini mushrooms, sliced ¼ inch thick (about 3 cups)

2 garlic cloves, finely chopped

½ teaspoon kosher salt

Freshly ground black pepper

1 medium leek (white part only), cut into ¼-inch-thick half-moons (about 1 cup)

2 store-bought naan breads (each roughly 6 inches in diameter)

4 tablespoons mascarpone cheese

2 tablespoons finely grated Parmesan cheese

½ cup lightly packed grated Fontina cheese

White truffle oil, for drizzling

1 tablespoon chopped fresh flat-leaf parsley

Whenever he has an opportunity to cook for the family, Nate can get pretty creative. He's definitely an experimental cook. One time I witnessed him adding vodka and melted chocolate to a pot of some sort of Mexican quinoa casserole. "It's like a mole sauce," he claimed. (I thought it was awful, but he disagreed.) He also likes adding sriracha to pasta sauce. (That one actually works.) Right or wrong, he's fearless in the kitchen, and my favorite idea of his is using store-bought naan for pizzas. It's already a soft, pillowy base that holds up well to any toppings. Sautéed mushrooms and leeks infused with truffle oil, combined with a melty Fontina cheese, transform this humble beginning into a restaurant-quality flatbread that's simple and quick to prepare.

1 Preheat the oven to 500°F.

2 In a large skillet, melt the butter over medium heat. Add the mushrooms, garlic, salt, and pepper to taste and cook, stirring frequently, until the mushrooms start to soften and release their liquid, about 3 minutes. Add the leek and stir until it has softened, another minute or two. Remove the pan from the heat and set aside.

3 Put the naan on a baking sheet and spread each with 2 tablespoons of the mascarpone cheese. Sprinkle 1 tablespoon Parmesan over the mascarpone on each, then add ¼ cup Fontina to each. Divide the mushroom mixture between the two breads.

4 Bake for 8 to 10 minutes, until the naan is golden brown on the edges and the cheese is bubbling. Transfer the pizzas to a cutting board, drizzle with a little bit of truffle oil, and garnish with chopped parsley. Cut each pizza into 4 pieces and serve immediately!

VIETNAMESE CARAMELIZED FISH (CA KHO TO)

SERVES 4 **TIME** 1 hour

FOR MARINATING THE FISH

3 tablespoons fish sauce

1 tablespoon sugar

1 medium shallot, minced

1 garlic clove, minced

½ teaspoon freshly ground black pepper

4 (8-ounce) bone-in fish steaks, 1½ inch thick (like catfish)

FOR COOKING THE FISH

2 tablespoons sugar

2 tablespoons extra-virgin olive oil

1 tablespoon minced shallots

2 garlic cloves, minced

¾ cup coconut water

1 teaspoon kosher salt

Sliced scallions (green parts only), for garnish

1 or 2 sliced Thai chile peppers, for garnish

Ca kho to is a Vietnamese traditional home-cooked comfort meal served over white rice with a downpour of caramelized sauce. Its bittersweet flavor is the perfect match for the tang of a tamarind-based soup (like my Vietnamese Vegetarian Tamarind Soup, page 97). I suggest catfish, halibut, cod, or sea bass for this recipe, because they have a great meaty texture, but if you aren't able to find them, use any firm-fleshed white fish.

1 **MARINATE THE FISH:** In a large bowl, whisk together the fish sauce, sugar, shallot, garlic, and black pepper. Add the fish steaks and turn gently to coat all the pieces thoroughly. Set aside to marinate for 20 minutes.

2 **COOK THE FISH:** In a Dutch oven, heavy-bottomed pot, or Vietnamese clay pot large enough to hold the fish steaks in a single layer, start by making a caramel Stir together the sugar and 2 tablespoons water. Place over medium-high heat and cook until the mixture turns a beautiful dark amber color on the bottom of the pot, 3 to 5 minutes. (Don't walk away—the timing will depend on your pot and your stove, so watch carefully.) As soon as the sugar is evenly brown, immediately whisk in the olive oil, reduce the heat to medium, then add the shallots and stir until fragrant, about 2 minutes. Add the garlic, stir for another minute, then gently add the fish steaks and any marinade left in the bowl. Add the coconut water and the salt and bring the liquid to a gentle boil. Reduce the heat to medium-low and continue cooking at a simmer until the sauce begins to thicken, 15 to 20 minutes.

3 Gently flip the fish over. The fish should be beautifully browned. Continue simmering on the second side until the sauce has reduced to a rich brown glaze, another 10 minutes. (It will be great as a sauce to serve over rice!) Plate the fish and garnish with sliced scallions and Thai chile peppers. (This is best eaten the same day.)

VEGGIE MU SHU

SERVES 4   **TIME** 30 minutes

FOR THE MU SHU SAUCE

¼ cup vegetable broth

¼ cup soy sauce

2 tablespoons orange juice

1 teaspoon rice vinegar

1 teaspoon sesame oil

1 teaspoon kosher salt

1 teaspoon cornstarch

FOR THE HOISIN DIPPING SAUCE

¼ cup hoisin sauce

1 tablespoon soy sauce

½ teaspoon sesame oil

FOR THE STIR-FRY

3 tablespoons neutral-tasting oil (such as avocado oil)

2 large eggs, whisked to blend

½ yellow onion, thinly sliced

2 garlic cloves, minced

1 teaspoon grated peeled fresh ginger

Half a (14-ounce) block firm tofu, cut into ½-inch-thick slabs about 1 × 3 inches

½ cup shredded carrots

¼ cup shredded fresh wood ear mushrooms (optional)

¼ cup sliced fresh shiitake mushrooms

2 scallions, cut into 2-inch lengths, each piece halved lengthwise

3 cups shredded green cabbage (from ½ medium head)

8 (10- or 12-inch) thin tortillas (such as cassava tortillas) or mandarin pancakes, warmed (see Heating Tortillas, page 59)

If Nate and I were to have a food baby (as opposed to the two human ones we have!), it would be this veggie mu shu. It's full of healthy Asian flavors (my contribution) and all wrapped up in a "tortilla" (Nate's offering). Nate's favorite food is a burrito, and his second favorite is anything wrapped in a tortilla, or, as he puts it, a "soft, warm food blanket." Maybe that's why I craved mu shu so much before Erisy was born? What I love most about it is the soft crunch from the shredded cabbage and savory mushroom filling. This one comes together really fast, and like so much homemade Chinese food, it's better than takeout. If you're tight on time, try buying preshredded carrots and coleslaw mix for this.

1 **MAKE THE MU SHU SAUCE:** In a small bowl, stir together the broth, soy sauce, orange juice, rice vinegar, sesame oil, salt, and cornstarch. Set aside.

2 **MAKE THE HOISIN DIPPING SAUCE:** In a small bowl, whisk together the hoisin, soy sauce, and sesame oil to blend. Set aside.

3 **MAKE THE STIR-FRY:** Heat a large wok over medium-high heat. Add 1 tablespoon of the oil, then add the eggs. Using a silicone spatula, stir and scrape the eggs off the bottom immediately, stirring for just a few seconds, until the eggs are fluffy and mostly set. (You don't want the eggs to look completely cooked, as they'll continue cooking after you remove them from the pan.) Transfer the eggs to a bowl and set aside.

4 Add another 1 tablespoon of the oil to the wok, then add the sliced onion and cook until the onion becomes translucent, about 1 minute. Add the garlic and ginger and stir-fry until fragrant, another minute. Add the tofu and stir-fry

until it gets lightly crisp, about 2 minutes. Transfer everything to a plate and set aside.

5 Add the remaining 1 tablespoon oil to the wok and toss in the carrots, wood ear mushrooms, shiitake mushrooms, and scallions and stir-fry over high heat until slightly wilted, about 2 minutes. Add the egg, tofu, and mu shu sauce to the wok and stir quickly to blend. Add the cabbage, remove the pan from the heat, and stir to coat the cabbage—the cabbage cooks super fast here, and the residual heat from the rest of the food will continue to cook it to a perfect crunch, so don't be tempted to cook it longer. (While the mu shu can be refrigerated for a day and reheated, it probably won't retain the same crunch.)

6 **TO ASSEMBLE:** Place a warm tortilla on a plate and spread some of the dipping sauce in the middle. Add as much or as little of the veggie mixture as you'd like and roll it up like a burrito. Enjoy with the remaining hoisin dipping sauce!

BUTTER CHICKEN CURRY

SERVES 4 **TIME** 1 hour

1 tablespoon garam masala

2 teaspoons ground cumin

1 teaspoon ground turmeric

½ teaspoon ground cardamom

½ teaspoon paprika

½ teaspoon ground cinnamon

½ teaspoon dried oregano

2 pounds boneless, skinless chicken thighs, quartered

3 tablespoons extra-virgin olive oil or ghee

½ medium onion, roughly chopped

4 garlic cloves, minced

2 teaspoons grated peeled fresh ginger

1 teaspoon kosher salt, plus more to taste

1 (15-ounce) can crushed tomatoes

4 tablespoons (½ stick) unsalted butter

1 cup full-fat canned coconut milk

1 bay leaf

1 teaspoon lemon juice, plus more to taste

I had some of the best Indian food when I worked at a tech company in Silicon Valley. My lovely coworkers would cater incredible meals from the best local Indian restaurants around Sunnyvale, which boasts a large Indian community. I was always partial to the butter chicken curry, or *murgh makhani,* full of saucy spice and belly-warming flavor. The chicken is so meltingly tender that every plate came back almost licked clean. Serve with steaming hot basmati rice or fresh naan on the side.

1 In a large bowl, stir together the garam masala, cumin, turmeric, cardamom, paprika, cinnamon, and oregano. Add the chicken and turn to coat all the pieces evenly with the spices. Set aside for 10 minutes.

2 Heat a Dutch oven or heavy-bottomed pot over medium-high heat. Add 2 tablespoons of the olive oil and the onion and cook, stirring frequently, until translucent and fragrant, about 3 minutes, adjusting the temperature as necessary. Add the garlic and ginger and cook for another minute, stirring.

3 Add the remaining 1 tablespoon oil to the pan, then add the chicken (and any leftover spices) and sprinkle with the salt. Cook for 5 minutes, turning the chicken halfway through when it releases easily from the pan, then add the crushed tomatoes, butter, coconut milk, bay leaf, and lemon juice. Reduce the heat to medium-low and let simmer, stirring occasionally, until the chicken is cooked through and tender, about 30 minutes. Season with additional salt and lemon juice, if desired. Serve immediately, or continue simmering until the sauce is thicker, if you prefer, then serve hot. (The chicken can also be cooled and refrigerated in the sauce for up to 3 days and reheated.)

TAMARIND-CUMIN GRILLED PORK CHOPS

SERVES 4 **TIME** 20 minutes, plus marinating time

2 tablespoons tamarind concentrate

2 tablespoons fish sauce

2 tablespoons extra-virgin olive oil

2 teaspoons ground cumin

1 teaspoon dark brown sugar

1 teaspoon sesame oil

4 garlic cloves, finely chopped

4 boneless pork loin chops (1 to 2 pounds, depending on preferred thickness)

¼ cup cold water

2 teaspoons cornstarch

Chopped fresh cilantro, for garnish

Chopped scallions (green parts only), for garnish

The flavorful dance between cumin and tamarind is the key to these juicy chops. Pork chops can be dry and boring on their own, but this unusual marinade guarantees every bite winds up juicy and tender. You can also use the sauce for grilling chicken, tofu, or steak.

1 In a bowl, mix together the tamarind concentrate, fish sauce, olive oil, cumin, brown sugar, sesame oil, and garlic. Add the pork chops, turn to coat them all evenly, and marinate for 30 minutes at room temperature, or cover and refrigerate for 2 hours (or overnight).

2 Heat a gas or charcoal grill to medium heat (about 400°F). When it's hot, brush the grates clean. Remove the pork chops from the marinade (reserve the marinade), letting any excess drip back into the bowl, and put the chops over direct heat. Grill (keeping the grill covered as much as you can) until the internal temperature reaches 145°F using a digital thermometer, 4 to 6 minutes for thinner chops or 8 to 10 minutes for thicker chops, turning once when the meat releases easily from the grill.

3 Meanwhile, in a small saucepan, whisk together the cold water and cornstarch until smooth. Add the reserved marinade, stir to blend, and bring to a boil over medium-high heat. Once the mixture boils and the liquid thickens to the consistency of gravy, remove it from the heat and set aside. (If it seems thick, you may want to add a tablespoon or two of water to thin it out.)

4 When the pork chops are cooked, smear some of the sauce over each one, garnish with chopped cilantro and scallions, and serve with any extra sauce alongside.

TAKE IT FROM ME Found Cuisine

Delicious pork chops are one of my favorite leftovers to find in the refrigerator. Use them as the base for a delicious bánh mì sandwich, or slice them and serve over ramen or in a quick stir-fry.

multipot Magic
LOW + SLOW
or PRESSURE-
COOKING

Whether your schedule demands a speedy meal or allows you to go low and slow, modern multipot technology can be your helping hand with dinner. I've learned that sauces, stews, and even risotto are a walk in the park for a multipot. Spoiler alert: You're going to have a new favorite way to make prime rib!

FRENCH ONION RISOTTO

SERVES 3 or 4 as a main dish or 6 to 8 as a side dish   **TIME** 1 hour

2 tablespoons unsalted butter

2 large yellow onions, halved and cut into ¼-inch-thick slices (about 4 cups)

2 teaspoons kosher salt, plus more for seasoning

1 teaspoon sugar

1 cup Arborio rice

1 teaspoon dried thyme

2 garlic cloves, minced

2¼ cups low-sodium beef stock or broth (or vegetable broth)

⅓ cup mascarpone cheese

½ cup grated Gruyère cheese, plus more for serving

Freshly ground black pepper (optional)

Let's combine the best parts of French onion soup and risotto into one recipe! Both would usually take hours to cook separately, but I like to let my multipot get it done in record time. What appears down inside the pot, after the steam escapes, is a luscious, creamy risotto tinged with a deep caramelized onion sweetness. Pair with a light green salad and a glass of pinot noir for a luxurious meal. Bon appétit!

1 Press the "sauté" button on the multipot and let the insert pot get hot. Add the butter. When the butter has melted and begins to bubble, add the onions, salt, and sugar. Let the onions cook, stirring occasionally, until they start to soften and release their liquid, about 3 minutes. Then, cook until the onions caramelize and get good and brown, another 12 to 16 minutes, stirring occasionally only when you see the onions start to brown. (It's okay to walk away for a minute or two here.)

2 When the bottom of the pot has an even brown layer and the onions have all turned brown, add the Arborio rice, thyme, and garlic. Stir to coat all the rice, then add the broth, stirring and scraping the pot to release any browned bits from the bottom. Cancel the "sauté" function.

3 Attach the lid of the multipot and turn the steam release handle to "sealing." Press the "pressure cook/manual" button, select high pressure, and set the cooking time for 10 minutes.

4 When the time is up, turn the steam release handle to "venting" to quick-release the pressure.

5 Open the pot, add the mascarpone and Gruyère cheeses, stirring until the mascarpone has melted and incorporating any delicious browned bits from the bottom of the pot. Season with salt and pepper (if using) to taste. Divide among bowls (or transfer to one big serving bowl), top with more shaved Gruyère, and enjoy!

LENTIL STEW *with* SWEET POTATOES AND KALE

SERVES 4 **TIME** 50 minutes

1 tablespoon extra-virgin olive oil

1 onion, chopped

1 large sweet potato (12 ounces), peeled and cut into ½-inch pieces (about 2 cups)

2 large stalks celery, cut into ½-inch pieces (about 1 cup)

3 garlic cloves, minced

2 teaspoons ground cumin

1 teaspoon ground turmeric

1 teaspoon dried thyme

½ teaspoon ground ginger

¼ teaspoon ground coriander

3 teaspoons kosher salt

4 cups vegetable broth

½ cup split red lentils

½ cup French green lentils

½ cup canned crushed tomatoes

2 cups packed chopped kale

¼ cup chopped fresh flat-leaf parsley, plus more for garnish

Juice of ½ lemon

Convert the health-food skeptics in your life with this nutty and hearty veggie stew. It's a nutritional powerhouse that's creamy and satisfying enough to be an indulgent meal, especially when paired with a crusty slice of country bread or naan.

1 Press the "sauté" button on the multipot and let the insert pot get hot. Add the olive oil, then add the onion and cook, stirring occasionally, until the onion is translucent, about 3 minutes. Add the sweet potato, celery, garlic, cumin, turmeric, thyme, ginger, coriander, and 2 teaspoons of the salt. Sauté until the celery is soft and the spices become super fragrant, another 3 minutes. Stir in the vegetable broth and 2 cups water. Add the red lentils, French green lentils, and crushed tomatoes. Cancel the "sauté" function.

2 Attach the lid to the multipot and turn the steam release handle to "sealing." Press the "pressure cook/manual" button, select high pressure, and set the cooking time for 13 minutes.

3 When the time is up, turn the steam release handle to "venting" to quick-release the pressure.

4 Open the pan and, with an immersion blender, give the stew a few quick pulses to puree just a bit of it—you want the sweet potatoes to be chunky, so just two or three pulses should do it. (You can also carefully transfer about 1 cup of the stew to a stand blender, blend until smooth, then return that portion to the pot.)

5 Stir in the kale, parsley, and lemon juice. Close the lid again and press the "pressure cook/manual" button. Select high pressure and set the cooking time for just 2 minutes.

6 When the time is up, turn the steam release handle to "venting" to quick-release the pressure.

7 Open and season with the remaining 1 teaspoon salt (or to taste). Serve topped with parsley. (The stew can also be cooled and refrigerated for up to 3 days and reheated.) Enjoy!

TAKE IT FROM ME Getting to Know Your Multipot

It's worth taking the time to get to know your multipot. Read the directions to learn what all the buttons and knobs do and, most importantly, how to be safe when you're pressure cooking. (True story. I burned my shin on the steam from the venting valve on one of my mother's machines when I was younger. I thought I was giving myself a "steam facial." Don't do this.) Here are a few crucial tips:

• Don't forget the liquid! One common mistake people make when cooking with a multipot is not adding enough liquid to bring to pressure.

• Multipots are very talkative. Learn what the beeps mean—like when the machine has come up to pressure and is starting the actual cooking time.

• There are two ways to let the steam out of the multipot when the cooking is finished. "Natural release" means letting the machine slowly release pressure on its own. "Quick release" means turning the steam release handle or venting knob to "vent" so that all the steam pressure releases immediately. (The food inside cooks longer if you allow the pressure to release naturally.) Many recipes call for a few minutes of natural release, followed by quick release.

VIETNAMESE CHICKEN CURRY

SERVES 6   **TIME** 40 minutes, plus marinating time

FOR THE CHICKEN

1 tablespoon Madras
curry powder

1 teaspoon onion powder

1 teaspoon garlic powder

1 teaspoon kosher salt

Freshly ground black pepper

1 pound boneless, skinless
chicken thighs

1 pound chicken drumsticks

FOR THE CURRY

2 tablespoons extra-virgin
olive oil

1 yellow onion, chopped

3 or 4 garlic cloves, minced,
to taste

1 tablespoon minced peeled
fresh ginger

1 (14-ounce) can full-fat
coconut milk (stirred if
separated)

1 cup low-sodium chicken broth

1¾ pounds Yukon Gold potatoes
(4 or 5), peeled and cut into
1-inch chunks

3 carrots, cut into 1-inch
chunks

2 stalks fresh lemongrass
(tender white inside parts only),
cut into 2-inch pieces

2 tablespoons Madras curry
powder

2 tablespoons fish sauce

1 tablespoon sugar

Kosher salt

This Vietnamese chicken curry is near and dear to my heart. It was a dish that my parents made for almost every ancestral celebration. It's often served with white rice or a light, crunchy Vietnamese baguette. My dad and my brother-in-law, Jason, bonded over this curry (and a couple beers). It's also Jason's favorite Vietnamese dish to order whenever we go out.

I'd describe Vietnamese curry as being slightly lighter and simpler than the rich Thai and Indian ones. It's seasoned with fish sauce, ginger, and garlic and finished with a light coconut creaminess.

1 PREPARE THE CHICKEN: In a large bowl, combine the curry powder, onion powder, garlic powder, salt, and pepper to taste. Add all the chicken and stir until completely coated. Let sit for at least 15 minutes while preparing the rest of the ingredients.

2 MAKE THE CURRY: Press the "sauté" button on the multipot and let the insert pot get hot. Add the olive oil and then the onion and cook, stirring frequently, until the onion begins to brown, 6 to 8 minutes. Add the garlic, ginger, and the chicken. Mix well. Add half the coconut milk, the broth, potatoes, carrots, lemongrass, curry powder, fish sauce, and sugar and mix gently to combine.

3 Attach the lid to the multipot and turn the steam release handle to "sealing." Press the "meat/stew" button and set the cooking time for 12 minutes.

4 When the time is up, turn the steam release handle to "venting" to quick-release the pressure. When you're ready to eat, pour in the rest of the coconut milk. Stir gently and season with salt to taste. (The curry can also be cooled and refrigerated, covered, for up to 3 days and reheated.) Enjoy!

TIPS FOR BUZY LIVES Sounds Appealing

Short on time? Don't peel the potatoes and carrots. The skins are perfectly edible, and there's no compromise in flavor or texture.

NATE'S TURKEY MEATBALLS

SERVES 2 to 4 **TIME** 1 hour

1 pound ground turkey (thigh meat preferred, if available)

½ cup finely grated Parmesan cheese

¼ cup quick-cooking oats

1 large egg

1 tablespoon chopped fresh flat-leaf parsley

1 tablespoon chopped fresh basil

1 teaspoon fish sauce

1 teaspoon garlic powder

1 teaspoon dried oregano

1 teaspoon kosher salt

½ teaspoon onion powder

⅛ teaspoon red pepper flakes (optional)

4 tablespoons extra-virgin olive oil

1 (24-ounce) jar marinara sauce

12 ounces spaghetti or other pasta

Nate has always been "creative" in the kitchen. The first time he cooked for me, on our second or third date, I was served a burrito stuffed with boxed mac and cheese and hot dogs. There was also a bonus side of store-bought frozen party meatballs. I did my best to appear to enjoy his meal as he watched excitedly. Being in a new relationship, I didn't want to offend him, so I said, "Mmmmm!" while inside, I was secretly wondering how it would ever work. Fast-forward ten years and he's come a long way. His "advanced" version of meatballs is now made from scratch with ground turkey thigh meat, oats, herbs, and a splash of fish sauce, which is the secret ingredient here and a trick picked up from my dad. Our go-to marinara is Rao's Homemade, which Nate enhances with a hint of sriracha. Serve with pasta, zoodles, or spaghetti squash, or with my Cheesy Garlic Bread (page 197).

This recipe makes about 12 meatballs the size of golf balls.

1 In a large bowl, combine the turkey, Parmesan, oats, egg, parsley, basil, fish sauce, garlic powder, oregano, salt, onion powder, and red pepper flakes (if using) by hand until thoroughly blended. Using a 1½- or 2-inch cookie scoop, form the mixture into meatballs and transfer to a plate. (They'll cook through at any size, so make the size you want.)

2 Press the "sauté" button on the multipot and let the insert pot get hot. Drizzle in 2 tablespoons of the olive oil. When the oil shimmers, add about 6 meatballs to the pan and brown them for 2 to 3 minutes per side, turning them only when they release easily from the pan. (These meatballs are super tender but also a little fragile, so don't pull on them if they don't want to move yet.) Gently transfer the meatballs to a plate. Add another 1 tablespoon of the oil to the pan and repeat with more meatballs. Repeat again with the remaining meatballs, adding the last tablespoon of the oil before browning. (You might not need the third batch if you made larger meatballs.) Cancel the "sauté" function.

3 Pour 2 cups of the marinara sauce into the insert pot, scraping up any browned bits off the bottom of the pot as you add the sauce, then gently add the meatballs to the pot, making sure not to squish them too much.

4 Attach the lid to the multipot and turn the steam release handle to "sealing." Press the "pressure cook/manual" button, select high pressure, and set the cooking time for 7 minutes.

5 When the time is up, let the pressure release naturally for 7 minutes, then turn the steam release handle to "venting" to quick-release the remaining pressure. (The meatballs can also be cooled and refrigerated for up to 3 days and reheated.)

6 Meanwhile, cook the pasta according to package directions. Drain and toss with the remaining marinara sauce.

7 Open the multipot and serve the meatballs over the hot spaghetti

TIPS FOR BUZY LIVES Skip a Step!

These meatballs are also delicious without the browning step—so if you'd like to save time or just make things a little easier, simply add the sauce to the olive oil in the insert pot and nestle the meatballs into the sauce!

PRESSURE COOKER CARNITAS

SERVES 4 to 6 **TIME** 1 hour 30 minutes

2 tablespoons extra-virgin olive oil

2 pounds boneless pork butt or pork shoulder, cut into 3-inch chunks

½ yellow onion, diced

5 garlic cloves, roughly chopped

2 teaspoons kosher salt

1 teaspoon ground cumin

1 teaspoon dried Mexican oregano

1 bay leaf

½ lemon, seeded

½ orange, seeded

¼ cup fresh cilantro, chopped

Freshly ground black pepper

1 cup low-sodium chicken broth

This is another one of Nate's originals that I've since made my own. He used to work as a freelance photographer and would start some mornings by piling pork shoulder into a pot and simmering it all day on the stove. A delicious waft of slow-cooked meat would hit me as I walked in after spending all day in the office. Now I use the more efficient multipot to get results that are just as aromatic. I'll braise the pork until extremely tender, then shred it into chunky bits and crisp them up under the broiler. Pile the meat into tacos with Cotija cheese, cilantro, and my Quick Pickled Red Onions (page 198); or layer it in a bowl of rice, beans, avocado, corn, and my Quick Chipotle Salsa (page 60). Or come to think of it, make nachos or sliders. However you end up eating the carnitas, they will be something to *tacobout*.

1 Press the "sauté" button on the multipot and let the insert pot get hot. Drizzle in the olive oil. Working in batches, sear 4 pieces of pork at a time, cooking about 3 minutes per side, or until all the pork is golden brown all over. Transfer seared pork to a plate and set aside. Repeat the process until all the pieces are seared. (You don't want to crowd them in the pot, so be patient here.) Cancel the "sauté" function.

2 Return all the pork to the pot, then add the onion, garlic, 1 teaspoon of the salt, the cumin, oregano, and bay leaf. Juice the lemon and orange over the meat, then drop the squeezed citrus shells in also. Add the cilantro and a generous grind of black pepper, then pour the broth all over everything to distribute the spices.

3 Attach the lid to the multipot and turn the steam release handle to "sealing." Press the "meat/stew"

button on high pressure and set the cooking time to 35 minutes.

4 When the time is up, let the pressure release naturally for 15 minutes, then turn the steam release handle to "venting" to quick-release any remaining pressure.

5 Position a rack 4 inches from the broiling unit and preheat the broiler. Line a rimmed baking sheet with foil.

6 Transfer the meat from the multipot to a bowl, drizzle with ½ cup of the juices from the pot, and season with the remaining 1 teaspoon salt. Shred the meat, mixing it with the juices as you go and adding a little more juice, if your meat looks dry. Spread the meat on the foil-lined baking sheet and broil for 3 to 4 minutes, until the top of the pork dries out and gets browned and crisp. (Watch carefully so it doesn't burn!) Enjoy!

Broiling the carnitas gives them the beautiful crunchy bits you love—but the effect doesn't really last in the fridge. If you'd like to make the carnitas a day or two ahead, allow the shredded, seasoned meat to cool in a bowl. Transfer to a sealed container and refrigerate up to 3 days. Right before you serve, spread the meat out on a foil-lined baking sheet and broil as directed.

TAKE IT FROM ME Worth the Search

Mexican oregano is a little more potent and flavorful than regular oregano, so look for it in the Hispanic foods section of a large grocery store, or even on Amazon.

KOREAN BRAISED SHORT RIBS (GALBIJJIM)

SERVES 4 **TIME** 1 hour 30 minutes

4 pounds beef short ribs, boneless short ribs, or chuck roast, cut into 3- to 4-inch pieces

1 large yellow onion, quartered

½ Korean pear, other Asian pear, or Red Delicious apple, chopped

7 garlic cloves, peeled

2 tablespoons minced fresh ginger

½ cup soy sauce

1 tablespoon kosher salt

2 tablespoons honey

2 tablespoons gochujang

½ cup kimchi (with juices)

¼ cup soju or sake

1 to 3 tablespoons gochugaru (or ¼ to ¾ teaspoon red pepper flakes), to taste

2 large carrots (about ¾ pound total), cut into 1-inch pieces

1 small daikon or Korean radish (about ¾ pound), peeled and cut into 1-inch chunks

1 russet or 2 Yukon Gold potatoes (about ¾ pound total), peeled and cut into 2-inch chunks

¼ cup thickly sliced scallions (green parts only)

1 tablespoon sesame oil

Toasted sesame seeds, for garnish

In LA's Koreatown there's always a long line flowing out the door of Sun Nong Dan, a 24-hour, cultlike, sweat-inducing cornerstone of the area. They're known for their *galbijjim*, a cauldron of spicy hot Korean braised short ribs, bubbling with potatoes, carrots, and onions (and a layer of melted cheese on top if you want). When I told my sister about my experience eating there, she couldn't wait to come visit. In the meantime, I sent her this recipe (after rounds of testing and enjoying it at home), and once she made it herself, she understood what I meant.

The cut of meat you choose to use is dependent on taste. Short ribs are fattier and more flavorful, boneless short ribs are meaty and convenient, and chuck roast is leaner but also winds up very tender! Also, the meat from these ribs is used in the amazing Korean Beef Hash (page 57).

1 Put the meat in a large bowl, add cold water to cover, and soak for 30 minutes. (This draws out impurities in the meat and loosens extra shards in the bone so they can be rinsed off.) Rinse and drain the meat and pat dry.

2 In a blender, combine the onion, pear, garlic, ginger, soy sauce, salt, honey, gochujang, kimchi and its juices, soju, and gochugaru. Blend until smooth.

3 In the insert pot of a multipot, stir together the meat and the sauce mixture until the meat is coated. Attach the lid to the multipot and turn the steam release handle to "sealing." Press the "meat/stew" on high pressure and set the cooking time for 30 minutes.

4 When the time is up, turn the steam release handle to "venting" to quick-release the pressure. Open and add the carrots, radish, and potato(es). Secure the lid again and turn the steam release handle to "sealing." Press the "meat/stew" on high pressure button again and set the cooking time for 8 minutes.

5 When the time is up, turn the steam release handle to "venting" to quick-release the pressure. Scoop the stew into a serving bowl. (You can also braise the ribs up to 3 days ahead and reheat in a pot over low heat on the stove before serving.) Garnish with scallions, a drizzle of sesame oil, and a sprinkling of sesame seeds.

SLOW-COOKED PORK FOR BÁNH MÌ SANDWICHES

SERVES 6 **TIME** 45 minutes, plus 8 hours slow cooking

FOR THE PORK

1 tablespoon Chinese five-spice powder

1 tablespoon dark brown sugar

1 tablespoon kosher salt

1½ teaspoons freshly ground black pepper

2 pounds boneless pork shoulder or pork butt

3 tablespoons neutral-tasting oil (such as avocado oil)

½ cup soy sauce

2 tablespoons hoisin sauce

1 tablespoon minced fresh ginger

1 teaspoon sesame oil

6 garlic cloves, minced

FOR THE SANDWICHES

1 cup mayonnaise (preferably Kewpie)

¼ cup sriracha

2 small or 1 large baguette, sliced for 6 sandwiches, or similar hearty 6-inch rolls

Pickled Carrots and Daikon (page 198)

½ white onion, very thinly sliced

½ English cucumber, halved lengthwise, then cut on the diagonal into ¼-inch-thick slices

12 sprigs fresh cilantro

1 or 2 jalapeños, thinly sliced (optional)

Many of my friends growing up had taco Tuesdays or Friday night pizzas every week. We had bánh mì Fridays! My parents worked long hours and my sister and I had piano lessons every Friday evening in downtown San Jose, California. Since they didn't have time to cook, my parents would stop by a tiny shack for a quick dinner before we faced our teacher. It was the *best* bánh mì in town. I always asked for the classic ham and pâté, while my sister went for the Vietnamese grilled pork. And back then a sub was only 75¢! I remember being shocked a few years later to see the price had been increased to $5.

Bánh mì are now everywhere. Besides pork and pâté, you can find them in many incredible Asian-inspired variations. Here I start by rubbing a pork shoulder with five-spice, caramelizing it, then cooking it until it becomes fall-apart tender. You have the option of cooking it fast or slow in the multipot. If you can't find the light Vietnamese baguettes, use a French baquette or ciabatta rolls. You could also pile the pork into sliders with the usual spicy sriracha aioli, cilantro, sliced jalapeños, onions, and pickles.

1 **PREPARE THE PORK:** In a small bowl, mix together the five-spice powder, brown sugar, salt, and black pepper. Generously rub the mixture all over the pork.

2 Press the "sauté" button on the multipot and let the insert pot get hot. Add the neutral oil, then sear the pork on all four sides until the pork has a nice brown crust and releases easily from the pan when you turn it with tongs, 3 to 5 minutes per side. (It's okay if the sugar burns a little in the pan.)

3 In another bowl, stir together the soy sauce, hoisin, ginger, sesame oil, and garlic. Pour the sauce into the insert pot of a multipot (or into a slow cooker) and place the pork on top.

4 Cover the multipot with a glass lid (or if using the regular lid, be sure to set the steam release handle to "venting"). Press the "slow cook" button, set to low pressure, and set the cooking time for 8 hours.

5 When the time is up, shred the pork directly in the liquid in the pot, so the pork absorbs the juices. It should be fall-apart tender. (If you're saving the pork for later, refrigerate the shredded meat up to 3 days, then reheat it in a skillet over medium heat, until it's heated through completely, before serving.)

6 **TO ASSEMBLE SANDWICHES:** In a small bowl, stir together the mayonnaise and sriracha. Spread about 2 tablespoons of the mayonnaise on each side of the baguettes (or to taste), then add a generous helping of shredded pork with all the juices to the bottom side of each sandwich. Top with pickled carrots and daikon, onion, cucumber, cilantro, and jalapeños, and serve immediately.

HONEY-SOY GLAZED RIBS

SERVES 4 to 8 **TIME** 50 minutes, plus marinating time

Like many trendy restaurants, my ribs are fused with Asian elements. I start with a dry spice rub to lock in the ribs' flavor and to help retain their moisture. Then I lather them with a thick honey-soy glaze to make them finger lickin' good.

FOR THE RIBS

2 racks baby back ribs
(3 to 4 pounds each)

2 tablespoons dark brown sugar

1 tablespoon kosher salt

1 tablespoon garlic powder

1 teaspoon freshly cracked
black pepper

1 teaspoon Chinese five-spice
powder

1 teaspoon smoked paprika

1 teaspoon ground ginger

FOR THE HONEY-SOY GLAZE

½ cup soy sauce

½ cup hoisin sauce

½ cup honey

2 tablespoons lime juice

2 teaspoons kosher salt

2 teaspoons sesame oil

2 teaspoons finely grated
peeled fresh ginger

4 garlic cloves, finely minced

½ teaspoon Chinese five-spice
powder

2 scallions (green parts only),
finely chopped, for garnish

Toasted sesame seeds, for
garnish

1 PREPARE THE RIBS: Rinse the ribs and remove the membrane, which is the thin layer of clear tissue that runs along the bony side of the ribs. (You can slide a small knife underneath it at one end and then just pull the membrane off—but note that some ribs may already have it removed.) Place the ribs on a baking sheet.

2 In a small bowl, mix together the brown sugar, salt, garlic powder, pepper, five-spice, paprika, and ginger. Sprinkle the rub onto the meat and rub it in on all sides. Set the ribs aside to sit for 1 hour at room temperature, or if you have time, for maximum flavor, cover the ribs and refrigerate them overnight.

3 Add ½ cup water to the insert pot of the multipot and place the trivet rack (that comes with each machine) inside. Cut each rib in half or in thirds, so that all the ribs fit sideways (with the bones vertical) inside the pot.

4 Attach the lid to the multipot and turn the steam release handle to "sealing." Press the "pressure cook/manual" button, select high pressure, and set the cooking time to 25 minutes. (If the ribs seem extra thick and meaty, set the timer for 30 minutes.)

5 MEANWHILE, MAKE THE HONEY-SOY GLAZE: In a

saucepan, stir together the soy sauce, hoisin, honey, lime juice, salt, sesame oil, ginger, garlic, and five-spice. Whisk until smooth, then bring the mixture to a boil over high heat. Reduce the heat to medium and let simmer for a few minutes to thicken to the consistency of ketchup.

6 When the rib cooking time is up, turn the steam release handle to "venting" to quick-release the pressure.

7 Transfer the ribs to a foil-lined baking sheet, meat-side up. (If you want to make the ribs a day ahead, you can let them cool on the baking sheet, then refrigerate overnight, covered. Let the ribs come to room temperature and proceed to the broiling step the next day.)

8 Position a rack in the center of the oven and preheat the oven's broiler. Transfer about ¼ cup of the honey-soy glaze to a bowl and brush the ribs on both sides with the sauce. Broil the ribs for about 5 minutes, rearranging the ribs if they're not browning evenly, until all the ribs are nice and browned and the sauce is bubbling.

9 Remove the ribs from the oven and brush on another layer of the honey-soy glaze. Garnish with scallions and sesame seeds, and serve with the remaining glaze for dipping.

FAST OR SLOW LAMBCHETTA

SERVES 4 to 6 **TIME** 30 minutes, plus 6 hours slow cooking or 1 hour pressure cooking

¼ cup fresh flat-leaf parsley leaves

¼ cup fresh rosemary leaves

¼ cup fresh sage leaves

¼ cup fresh basil leaves

4 tablespoons extra-virgin olive oil

1 tablespoon fresh thyme leaves

4 garlic cloves, peeled

Grated zest and juice of 1 lemon (reserve the lemon "shells")

1 tablespoon kosher salt, plus more for seasoning

2 teaspoons fennel seeds

½ teaspoon red pepper flakes

2½ pounds boneless lamb shoulder roast, butterflied (see Note)

Freshly ground black pepper

½ cup low-sodium chicken broth

Porchetta is a beautifully bound and rolled Italian pork roast that's shockingly tender after a pressure cooker session. I'm shaking things up by swapping the pork for lamb and coloring it with a smattering of pungent herbs and squeezes of citrus, which will dial down the more gamey lamb flavor. This lambchetta melts in your mouth whether cooked fast (in a pressure cooker) or slow (in a slow cooker). Pair this with Quinoa Pilaf with Curry Miso Dressing (page 179) and the Spring Farro and Veggie Salad (page 75) for a special holiday meal.

1 In a food processor, blend together the parsley, rosemary, sage, basil, 2 tablespoons of the olive oil, the thyme, garlic, lemon zest, lemon juice, salt, fennel seeds, and red pepper flakes until it becomes a paste.

2 Butterfly the lamb and lay it flat on a cutting board, fat-side down. (The bottom portion may not be entirely covered in fat, but you want the red meat side facing up.) Evenly distribute the paste on top of the lamb and then roll it up, starting from a short end, so that the fattiest side of the lamb winds up on the outside of the roll. Using kitchen twine, tie the lamb at four or five evenly spaced intervals. Season the roll with salt and pepper.

3 **TO SLOW-COOK:** Heat a large cast-iron pan over high heat. Add the remaining 2 tablespoons olive oil. When the oil begins to smoke, sear the meat on all sides until golden brown, 3 to 4 minutes per side. Transfer the lamb and the juices to a slow cooker. Add the chicken broth and the reserved lemon shells.

4 Cover the slow cooker with a glass lid. Cook on low heat for 6 hours. When the cooking has finished, slice and serve the lamb.

5 **TO COOK IN A MULTIPOT:** Press the "sauté" button on the multipot and let the insert pot get hot. Add the remaining 2 tablespoons olive oil. When the oil begins to smoke, sear the meat on all sides until golden brown, about 5 minutes per side. Cancel the "sauté" function. Add the chicken broth and the reserved lemon shells to the insert pot.

6 Attach the lid to the multipot and turn the steam release handle to "sealing." Press the "pressure cook/manual" button, select high pressure, and set the cooking time for 45 minutes. When the time is up, turn the steam release handle to "venting" to quick-release the pressure. Let the lamb rest for 15 minutes, then slice and serve.

Note Butterflying is simply the process of cutting and flattening a large piece of meat so it can be rolled up around a filling. Ask your butcher to butterfly the lamb for you if you don't want to do it yourself.

JAPANESE BEEF CURRY

SERVES 3 or 4   **TIME** 1 hour 10 minutes

4 tablespoons (½ stick) unsalted butter

¼ cup all-purpose flour

2 tablespoons S&B curry powder

1½ teaspoons garam masala

1 tablespoon extra-virgin olive oil

1½ pounds beef stew meat, patted dry with paper towels

1 medium onion, quartered and sliced into ½-inch-thick pieces

2 cups low-sodium chicken broth

1 tablespoon soy sauce

1 tablespoon ketchup

1 tablespoon Worcestershire sauce

1 tablespoon honey

2 garlic cloves, minced

1 teaspoon minced peeled fresh ginger

1 teaspoon kosher salt

2 carrots, cut into ¾-inch chunks

3 medium Yukon Gold potatoes (about 1 pound), peeled and cut into 1-inch pieces

In college I loved those boxed Japanese curry squares where you just add water and whatever fresh ingredients you wanted. It was such a great semi-homemade shortcut that I didn't bother to find out how easy a made-from-scratch curry was until much later. But now, I never go back! With just a few simple ingredients, the curry paste is easy to make in your multipot. This curry features beef, carrots, potatoes, and onions, so it's hearty enough as its own meal. But add a side of rice and pickled ginger, or some Gochujang Bok Choy with Shiitake Mushrooms (page 187) to fill it out.

Look for S&B curry powder, a Japanese product, and garam masala, which is an Indian spice blend, in the spice section of an Asian market.

1 Press the "sauté" button on the multipot and let the insert pot get hot. Add the butter to the pot. When the butter has melted, sprinkle in the flour and cook for 1 minute, stirring constantly, then add the curry powder and garam masala. Stir until the mixture becomes a thick paste or roux, then transfer the paste to a bowl and set aside.

2 Add the olive oil to the pot, then about half the beef, and cook until the meat is browned on all sides, turning occasionally, about 5 minutes. Transfer the beef to a plate and repeat with the remaining beef. Add the onion, return all the beef to the pan, and cook until the onion is soft and beginning to brown, about 5 minutes more. Cancel the "sauté" function.

3 Add the chicken broth, soy sauce, ketchup, Worcestershire sauce, honey, garlic, ginger, salt, and reserved curry roux to the pot and stir to mix everything well with the meat. Attach the lid to the multipot and turn the steam release handle to "sealing." Press the "meat/stew" button and set the cooking time to 18 minutes.

4 When the time is up, turn the steam release handle to "venting" to quick-release the pressure. Open and stir in the carrots and potatoes, scraping the bottom of the pot to make sure nothing is sticking. Reattach the lid and set to "venting." Press the "meat/stew" button again and set the cooking time to 6 minutes.

5 When the time is up, turn the steam release handle to "venting" to quick-release the pressure. When you're ready to eat, remove the lid. (The curry can also be cooled and refrigerated for up to 3 days and reheated.) Enjoy!

SMOKY SLOW-COOKER CHILI

SERVES 4   **TIME** 15 minutes, plus slow cooking time

FOR THE CHILI

1 tablespoon extra-virgin olive oil

1 yellow onion, diced

1 pound ground beef (85 to 90% lean)

Kosher salt

1 cup low-sodium beef broth

1 (15-ounce) can diced fire-roasted tomatoes

1 (15-ounce) can tomato sauce

1 (12-ounce) bottle dark hoppy beer (such as a Double IPA)

3 tablespoons chili powder

2 teaspoons garlic powder

2 teaspoons ground cumin

2 teaspoons smoked paprika

2 teaspoons Worcestershire sauce

1 teaspoon cayenne pepper

2 (15-ounce) cans dark kidney beans, rinsed and drained

FOR SERVING

Sour cream

Chopped scallions (green parts only)

Red onions, diced

Shredded cheddar cheese

Who doesn't love a hearty chili, especially in the fall during football season? Yay, go sports! Whatever your favorite game to watch, I think we can all agree that adding smoked paprika and a hoppy IPA heightens standard game-day chili into the champion of spicy national stews. Serve straight out of the slow cooker with corn chips or corn bread.

1 **MAKE THE CHILI:** Press the "sauté" button on the multipot and let the insert pot get hot. Add the olive oil and heat until it glistens. Add the onion and cook, stirring, until translucent, about 3 minutes. Add the ground beef and a pinch of kosher salt and cook, stirring occasionally, until browned, 5 to 7 minutes. Cancel the "sauté" function. (If you're using a regular slow cooker, cook the onion and beef in a large cast-iron pot over medium-high heat, then transfer the beef and onions to the cooker.)

2 Add the beef broth, fire-roasted tomatoes, tomato sauce, beer, chili powder, garlic powder, cumin, smoked paprika, Worcestershire sauce, cayenne, and 1 teaspoon salt and stir to mix. Cover the multipot with a glass lid (or if using the regular lid, be sure to set the steam release handle to "venting"). Cook on the "slow cook" setting on low heat for 6 hours. (You can proceed, or let the multipot or regular slow cooker keep the chili warm for a few hours here.)

3 Ten minutes before serving, stir in the beans and let the chili sit to warm the beans through. (If you want to make the chili ahead, you can let it cool to room temperature here and then reheat before serving, or refrigerate the chili for up to 3 days before reheating.) Serve topped with sour cream, scallions, red onions, and cheddar.

PRESSURE COOKER PRIME RIB

SERVES 8 to 10   **TIME** 1 hour 30 minutes

2 tablespoons kosher salt

1 tablespoon garlic powder

1 tablespoon onion powder

1 tablespoon freshly ground black pepper

1 teaspoon sugar

½ teaspoon dried oregano

¼ teaspoon cayenne pepper

¼ teaspoon dried sage

1 (5-pound) boneless prime rib roast, tied, left at room temperature for 1 hour before cooking

1 cup low-sodium beef broth

2 tablespoons neutral-tasting oil (such as avocado oil)

1 tablespoon all-purpose flour

Prime rib is the star of our Christmas table every year. When we first began this tradition, more than a decade ago, it wasn't a meal I necessarily looked forward to making because it can be complicated to plan everything around its lengthy, oven-hogging cook time. Never again though, now that I have my trusty pressure cooker! The only thing I do is assemble the rub and let the multipot handle the big job, leaving the oven available for amazing sides like Tartiflette (page 188) or Crispy Brussels Sprouts with Chile-Lime-Garlic Sauce (page 191). Expect a juicy, tender showstopper every time. Save the leftover juices in the pot for making a rich gravy to serve over the beef.

Ask your butcher to trim and tie the meat for you. And if you don't see a boneless prime rib in the case, just ask—they can usually cut one for you on the spot!

1 In a small bowl, stir together the salt, garlic powder, onion powder, black pepper, sugar, oregano, cayenne, and sage. Generously rub the seasoning all over the meat, patting it into the cracks and onto the ends well.

2 Pour the beef broth into the multipot's insert pot. Place the trivet rack into the pot and put the roast on top, fat-side up. Attach the lid to the multipot and turn the knob to "sealing." Press the "pressure cook/manual" button, select high pressure, and set the cooking time for 6 minutes for a rare roast. (Set it for 7 minutes for medium-rare as shown here, or 8 minutes for medium.)

3 When the time is up, do not vent the steam knob. Let the pressure release naturally for 35 minutes.

4 Use the rack to transfer the meat to a platter, then pour the cooking liquid (about 1¼ cups) from the insert pot into a bowl and set aside.

5 Press the "sauté" button on the multipot and let the insert pot get hot. Add the oil to the pot, then sear the roast on each side for about 5 minutes, until nicely browned on all sides, about 20 minutes total. Remove the roast and let rest for 10 minutes.

6 While the roast rests, make the jus: Sprinkle the flour into the pot and stir to mix with the remaining fat in the bottom of the pot. Add the reserved cooking liquid and whisk until the mixture bubbles and thickens. Add 1 cup water and whisk until smooth. (You can strain the sauce if you prefer it to be completely smooth.) Serve the roast immediately, carved as desired, with the sauce on the side.

SIDE-KICKS

We all need them

Meals can't truly be complete without the side dishes. An entrée is even more special with a good sidekick, like flavorful veggies, tart and pickled bites, crispy potatoes, or cheesy bread. Here's my list of sides, appetizers, and condiments to enhance your delicious meals.

QUINOA PILAF *with* CURRY-MISO DRESSING

SERVES 6 to 8   **TIME** 25 minutes

1 tablespoon extra-virgin olive oil

1 cup quinoa, rinsed

Curry-Miso Dressing (recipe follows)

1 cup shredded carrot

½ cup dried cherries or cranberries

¼ cup sliced almonds

1 (15-ounce) can chickpeas, rinsed and drained

2 scallions (green parts only), chopped

Kosher salt and freshly ground black pepper

This pilaf is chock-full of fruit, nuts, and vegetables. But aside from its diverse textures, the balance between the curry and miso flavors is what makes it unique.

1 In a heavy-bottomed pot with a lid, heat the olive oil over medium-high heat. Add the rinsed quinoa and let it toast for about 3 minutes, stirring frequently. Pour in 2 cups water and bring the mixture to a boil. Once the liquid has reduced down to the level with the quinoa (this will depend on the size of your pot, but it should take about 3 minutes), reduce the heat to its lowest setting and cover the pot. Let the quinoa cook until the liquid has been completely absorbed, another 5 to 7 minutes. Remove the pan from the heat and fluff the quinoa with a fork.

2 In a large bowl, combine the dressing, carrot, cherries, almonds, chickpeas, and scallions. Add the warm quinoa and mix well, seasoning to taste with salt and pepper as you go. Serve immediately, or let come to room temperature and refrigerate, covered, up to 3 days.

CURRY-MISO DRESSING

MAKES about ½ cup   **TIME** 5 minutes

¼ cup extra-virgin olive oil

2 tablespoons rice vinegar

1 tablespoon white or red miso

2 teaspoons minced fresh ginger

2 garlic cloves, minced

1 teaspoon honey

1 teaspoon kosher salt

1 teaspoon curry powder

¼ teaspoon ground cumin

I always keep a jar of curry-miso dressing ready in the refrigerator, where it will stay fresh for a week. It works over a crunchy grain bowl or lettuce salad, over fresh grilled chicken, or even as a stir-fry sauce for soba noodles.

In a small bowl, whisk together the olive oil, vinegar, miso, ginger, garlic, honey, salt, curry powder, and cumin to blend.

CHOOSE YOUR OWN ADVENTURE: SPRING ROLLS

SERVES 4 to 6 **TIME** 1½ hours

FOR THE PORK

½ pound pork loin (in one piece)

1 teaspoon kosher salt

FOR THE PEANUT SAUCE

½ cup salted peanut butter

2 tablespoons hoisin sauce

2 tablespoons soy sauce

1 tablespoon honey

1 tablespoon lime juice

1 garlic clove, peeled

½-inch knob fresh ginger

Chili-garlic sauce (optional)

FOR THE ROLLS

12 dried rice paper rounds (bán tráng)

12 pieces green leaf lettuce (or other greens), torn into roughly 4 × 2-inch pieces

4 cups cooked thin rice vermicelli

6 sprigs fresh mint

6 sprigs fresh shiso

6 sprigs fresh Thai basil or basil

6 sprigs fresh Vietnamese coriander (rau ram)

6 sprigs fresh cilantro

12 garlic chives (or a large handful)

15 medium (21/25) shrimp, cooked, tails removed, halved lengthwise

Have you ever heard of a spring roll bar? My parents used to have them whenever they had friends and family over for a party. The guests would assemble their own rolls, picking whatever fillings they wanted to wrap up. There would always be the typical pork loin, shrimp, and Vietnamese Grilled Pork Noodle Salad (see page 110), but sometimes they could find Grilled Salmon with Tamarind Dipping Sauce (page 132) or even crab sticks (usually for the kids). And then there'd be a multitude of fresh herbs from the backyard, which my dad grew proudly—fragrant Thai basil and mint, leafy cilantro, and spicy Vietnamese coriander. Below are many options for you to explore, alone or with a crowd. Choose your own spring roll adventure.

1 **COOK THE PORK:** Fill a pot just large enough to fit the pork about halfway with water, then bring to a boil over high heat. Reduce the heat to medium, then add the pork loin and the salt and simmer until the pork is cooked through, 15 to 18 minutes. (Make sure not to overcook it, as this will dry out the meat.) Transfer the meat to a cutting board to cool for about 10 minutes, then slice it into ⅛-inch-thick pieces.

2 **MEANWHILE, MAKE THE PEANUT SAUCE:** In a blender, whirl together the peanut butter, hoisin, soy sauce, honey, lime juice, garlic, ginger, and 2 tablespoons water until smooth. (Depending on your peanut butter, you may want to add a bit more water, a tablespoon at a time, so that the sauce is easy to dip into—the sauce should relax quickly to the bottom of the work bowl when the blade stops spinning.) Transfer to a bowl, top with a dollop of chili-garlic sauce (if desired), and set aside until ready to serve.

3 **SET UP THE ROLLS:** Arrange all the roll ingredients, including the pork, on a few plates on a large, clean work surface. Fill a pie pan about halfway with warm water and set it next to a clean cutting board or a large plate. Have a serving platter ready.

4 To make the rolls, dip a rice paper round into the warm water, rotating it just until the surface is wet. (Don't let it sit too long, or it'll become extremely sticky and hard to work with. While the rice paper doesn't soften immediately, it will continue softening after you take it out of the water.) Transfer the round to the cutting board or a plate. Place a piece of lettuce in the lower third of the round, then pile about ¼ cup cooked rice noodles and the leaves only from the five different kinds of herbs on top of the lettuce. Fold the round up and over the greens and noodles until the bottom edge of the round reaches the center, then fold in both sides of the round, like you're folding a burrito, and roll

(recipe continues)

once more to secure the greens and noodles inside. You should still have about 4 inches of rice paper flat on the cutting board. Place a long garlic chive into the place where the rolled paper meets the flat paper (the chive will stick out of one end of the roll), then place 2 or 3 shrimp halves (cut-sides up) next to the chive, on the unrolled portion of the paper. Place a strip or two of the pork on top of the shrimp, then continue rolling until the chive, shrimp, and pork are also sealed inside the spring roll. (Traditionally, the chive is left long, but I like to trim it off about 1 inch away from the end of the spring roll.) Continue making rolls until you've used all the ingredients. Serve immediately, with the peanut sauce for dipping.

GARLIC AND CHILI ROASTED SWEET POTATOES

SERVES 4 **TIME** 30 minutes

1 pound sweet potatoes, skin on, halved and cut lengthwise into ½-inch-thick slabs

3 tablespoons extra-virgin olive oil

1 teaspoon kosher salt

1 teaspoon garlic powder

1 teaspoon chili powder

I'm extremely partial to potatoes. I'll eat them in whatever shape or form, in any variety, with whatever seasoning. And I've been really into sweet potatoes now, more than ever. They're just as satisfying as regular potatoes, and because of the high fiber content, they keep me fuller longer. The crispy roasted chunks with their sweet fluffy flesh will absorb a dash of chili powder and garlic, making this recipe an exquisite side to the Pan-Seared Steak with Ssamjang Glaze (page 135) or a colorful addition to the Rainbow Grain Bowl (page 123).

1 Preheat the oven to 400°F. Line a rimmed baking sheet with foil.

2 In a large bowl, stir together the potatoes, olive oil, salt, garlic powder, and chili powder until the potatoes are evenly coated. Transfer the potatoes to the prepared baking sheet and bake for 22 to 25 minutes, turning the potatoes halfway through, until browned and soft all the way through. Serve immediately.

TOMATOES PROVENÇALE

SERVES 4 to 8 **TIME** 40 minutes

2 tablespoons grated Parmesan cheese

1 small shallot, finely minced

1 garlic clove, minced

1 teaspoon finely chopped fresh flat-leaf parsley

1 teaspoon finely chopped fresh basil

¼ teaspoon dried thyme

½ cup regular bread crumbs

¼ cup plus 2 tablespoons extra-virgin olive oil

4 large firm-ripe tomatoes (about 2½ pounds), stemmed and halved through the equator

Kosher salt and freshly ground black pepper

When I was in grade school, I owned just one cookbook, and it was all about how to cook with the microwave. My parents gave it to me because they saw that I loved to cook but didn't want me to tinker with the stove or oven at just seven or eight years old. The book contained a simple instruction for a "baked" tomatoes dish. I remember being so inspired after my very first solo cooking adventure that I re-created it many times. My tomatoes Provençale here is an adult version, where I use soft, ripened tomatoes with toasted bread crumbs mixed with cheese and herbs, all baked in a real oven. I recommend pairing this dish with a summer barbecue or my Fast or Slow Lambchetta (page 170).

Look for tomatoes that are ripe but still firm, because you want them to hold their shape in the oven. When they're in season, I love using heirloom tomatoes.

1 Preheat the oven to 400°F.

2 In a bowl, stir together the Parmesan, shallot, garlic, parsley, basil, and thyme. Add the bread crumbs and ¼ cup of the olive oil and blend until the mixture is evenly moist.

3 Drizzle the remaining 2 tablespoons olive oil across the bottom of a rimmed baking sheet or baking dish large enough to hold all the tomato halves, cut-sides up. Add the tomatoes and sprinkle the cut sides with salt and pepper. Spread about 2 tablespoons of the bread crumb mixture onto each tomato (more for larger tomatoes, less for smaller ones).

4 Bake for 22 to 25 minutes, until the tomatoes have softened and the bread crumb mixture is golden brown. Serve immediately.

GOCHUJANG BOK CHOY *with* SHIITAKE MUSHROOMS

SERVES 4 **TIME** 15 minutes

1 tablespoon gochujang

1 tablespoon soy sauce

1 tablespoon oyster sauce

1 teaspoon rice vinegar

1 teaspoon honey

1 teaspoon sesame oil

2 garlic cloves, minced

1 teaspoon finely chopped or grated peeled fresh ginger

1 tablespoon neutral-tasting oil (such as avocado oil)

10 shiitake mushrooms, stems discarded, caps halved (about 1 cup)

1 pound baby bok choy, quartered lengthwise

Bok choy is a popular ingredient in Asian cooking and requires very little preparation and cooks quickly. When combined with meaty shiitake mushrooms and a simple gochujang sauce, the crisp, cabbage-like vegetable transforms into a solid accompaniment to either my Japanese Beef Curry (page 172) or Orange Cauliflower Nuggets (page 136). Or add tofu and rice for a whole meal.

If you cook it longer than suggested below, bok choy can get quite watery, so you want to move quickly. Once it has wilted a little and is coated in the sauce, it's done.

1 In a bowl, whisk together the gochujang, soy sauce, oyster sauce, rice vinegar, honey, sesame oil, garlic, and ginger until the honey is incorporated. Set the sauce aside.

2 In a large wok, heat the neutral oil over high heat. When hot, toss in the shiitake mushrooms and stir fry for about 1 minute. Add the sauce, then add the bok choy and let it cook, stirring constantly to coat the vegetables in the sauce, just until the leaves have wilted, 2 to 3 minutes. Transfer to a serving plate and serve immediately.

TARTIFLETTE

SERVES 6 to 8 as a side dish or 4 as a main dish   **TIME** 1 hour

Kosher salt

3 large russet potatoes (about 2½ pounds), 2 peeled and 1 with skin on, cut into ½-inch chunks

4 tablespoons extra-virgin olive oil

½ yellow onion, chopped

1 cup packed baby spinach

3 garlic cloves, minced

Freshly ground black pepper

2 slices bacon, diced

¼ cup dry white wine (such as pinot grigio)

½ pound Brie cheese, cut into ¼-inch-thick slices (see Note)

This amazing cheesy potato bake is dedicated to my dear friend Aislin and her family. When she cooked it for a get-together, I was completely fascinated and just had to know how it was done. I love potatoes in every form, and this glorious potato gratin, baked with bacon and melted cheese, was new to me. She explained that every Sunday afternoon, she and her family would visit a local cheese and produce market in Mountain View, California, and take home some specialty items. A kind French man described *tartiflette*, with its special Reblochon cheese, to her eldest son, Caedon, and that was their introduction to this instant classic. With many tips and coaching from Aislin, here's my perfected *tartiflette* recipe that will delight and satisfy. I love serving *tartiflette* with a leafy green salad.

1 Preheat the oven to 400°F.

2 Bring a large pot of water to a boil and add 1 teaspoon salt. Add the potatoes and bring back to a boil. Boil for 5 minutes, then drain the potatoes thoroughly and set aside.

3 Oil the bottom of a 9 × 13-inch ceramic or metal baking dish with 2 tablespoons of the olive oil. Sprinkle the onion across the bottom of the pan, then add the spinach in an even layer.

4 In a bowl, combine the cooked potatoes with the remaining 2 tablespoons olive oil, the garlic, ½ teaspoon salt, and ground pepper

to taste. Mix to coat everything evenly, then add it to the baking dish, covering the spinach. Sprinkle the bacon evenly over the potatoes.

5 Transfer to the oven and bake for 30 to 35 minutes, until the liquid from the spinach has evaporated and the bacon is golden brown.

6 Remove the dish from the oven, pour the white wine over the top of everything, and place the Brie slices on top of the potatoes. (The Brie doesn't need to be sliced perfectly.) Return to the oven and bake for 5 minutes, until the cheese has melted. Enjoy!

Note A soft Brie cheese or Camembert (during the holidays) is more accessible than the traditional Reblochon.

CRISPY BRUSSELS SPROUTS
with CHILE-LIME-GARLIC SAUCE

SERVES 4 **TIME** 40 minutes

FOR THE BRUSSELS SPROUTS

1 pound medium Brussels sprouts (about the size of your thumb or a little bigger), trimmed and halved

2 tablespoons avocado oil

½ teaspoon kosher salt

Freshly ground black pepper

FOR THE SAUCE

1 teaspoon cornstarch

¼ cup packed dark brown sugar

2 tablespoons fish sauce

2 tablespoons rice vinegar

2 tablespoons lime juice

1 garlic clove, minced

½ teaspoon red pepper flakes, or to taste

Crisped to a golden-brown perfection and drizzled with a punchy, tangy sauce, these easy Brussels sprouts go seamlessly with Lemongrass Chicken Stir-Fry (page 131) or as a healthy topping in a rice or grain bowl. They're also an addictive bite-size snack for any time of the day that you can feel good about eating!

1 Position a rack in the bottom third of the oven and preheat the oven to 450°F. Line a rimmed baking sheet with foil and put the baking sheet in the oven to preheat. Let the pan heat in the oven for 10 minutes after the oven is hot.

2 **PREPARE THE BRUSSELS SPROUTS:** In a large bowl, combine the Brussels sprouts, oil, salt, and pepper to taste. Mix until each sprout is coated in the oil. Carefully remove the baking sheet from the oven and spread the Brussels sprouts evenly across the pan. Give the pan a shake to distribute them so they all have enough room to crisp up.

3 Return to the oven and bake the sprouts on the bottom rack for 20 to 25 minutes, stirring them around about halfway through cooking, until the Brussels sprouts are evenly golden brown and the leaves are dark and crispy.

4 **MEANWHILE, MAKE THE SAUCE:** In a small bowl, mix the cornstarch with 1 tablespoon water and set aside. In a small saucepan, combine the brown sugar, fish sauce, vinegar, and lime juice and stir over medium heat until the sugar dissolves. Add the garlic and red pepper flakes and bring to a boil. Reduce the heat to low, then give the cornstarch mixture a quick stir and pour it into the pan. Let the sauce come back to a boil, stirring until it becomes translucent again. Remove from the heat and set aside.

5 When the sprouts are done, carefully transfer them to a serving platter and drizzle the sauce on top (or serve it on the side). Enjoy!

TAKE IT FROM ME Get It Hot

The secret to the crispiness of these babies comes from the hot baking sheet itself. When you preheat the oven, line a rimmed baking sheet with foil and stick it in there as the oven heats, then let it continue heating for about 10 minutes once the oven is hot. The sizzling heat of the pan browns the vegetables and gives them a super lovely caramelized flavor. Don't limit this technique to Brussels sprouts—this recipe also works well with carrots, cauliflower, or broccoli!

FLAWLESSLY COOKED RICE

As in so many other Vietnamese families, rice had an important role at our table when I was growing up. Not one meal went by without it. I was taught to measure the correct amount of water using the "finger-dip method," where the water line above a layer of washed rice reached the first knuckle line on the index finger. For white rice, slightly below was best. For brown, slightly above the crease. It's hardly scientific, but it somehow seemed to work every time.

I have also included recipes for more than just plain rice. Enjoy the Coconut Rice with the Vietnamese Chicken Curry (page 159) or Lemongrass Chicken Stir-Fry (page 131), and the Tomato-Fried Rice with my Rockin' Beef Bowl (page 124).

WHITE RICE

MAKES about 4 cups   **TIME** 25 minutes

2 cups Calrose or jasmine rice

3 cups water

1 In a heavy-bottomed pot with a lid, rinse the rice with cool water until the water runs clear, then drain. Add the 3 cups water and bring to a boil over medium-high heat.

2 Reduce the heat to medium-low and let cook at a bare simmer until the liquid is almost absorbed, 8 to 12 minutes. Reduce the heat to extra low and cover with a lid. Let the rice steam for another 10 minutes, then remove from the heat. Fluff with a fork and serve.

PERFECT BROWN RICE

MAKES 3 cups   **TIME** 35 minutes

1 cup short-grain brown rice

2 cups water

1 In a heavy-bottomed pot with a lid, rinse the rice with cool water until the water runs clear, then drain. Add the 2 cups water and bring to a boil over high heat.

2 Reduce the heat to medium and let cook at a strong simmer until the liquid is almost absorbed, 15 to 18 minutes. Reduce the heat to extra low and cover with a lid. Let the rice steam for another 10 minutes, then remove from the heat. Fluff with a fork and serve.

COCONUT RICE

MAKES 3 cups **TIME** 30 minutes

1 cup jasmine rice

2 cups unsweetened coconut milk, from a carton

½ teaspoon sugar

Pinch of kosher salt

1 In a heavy-bottomed pot with a lid, rinse the rice with cool water until the water runs clear, then drain. Stir in the coconut milk, sugar, and salt and bring the mixture to a boil over medium-high heat.

2 Reduce the heat to medium and cook until the liquid is almost absorbed, 10 to 12 minutes. (Don't walk away here—you want to turn the heat down a tad if it threatens to boil over.) Cover the pot, reduce the heat to its lowest setting, and cook until the liquid is almost absorbed, 12 to 15 minutes. Fluff with a fork until any extra liquid is stirred in, and serve.

TOMATO-FRIED RICE

MAKES about 4 cups **TIME** 10 minutes

2 tablespoons ketchup

2 teaspoons soy sauce

1 teaspoon garlic powder

2 tablespoons unsalted butter

4 cups cold cooked white rice (day-old rice is best)

1 In a small bowl, mix together the ketchup, soy sauce, and garlic powder. Set aside.

2 In a large skillet or wok, melt the butter over medium-high heat. When the butter is completely melted, add the rice and cook,

stirring, until the grains have separated, 2 or 3 minutes. Add the ketchup mixture and continue to cook, stirring constantly, until each grain is covered with sauce, another minute or two. Transfer the rice to a serving platter.

TAKE IT FROM ME Tomato-Fried Macaroni

If you want a quick, inexpensive meal, do what I did as a kid—swap the rice out for about 3 cups cooked macaroni pasta. Now you have tomato mac!

TAKE IT FROM ME Rinsing Rice

When rice is packaged, it still has a thin layer of extra starch on the outside. Although it's perfectly safe to eat, it makes the rice extra sticky if you don't rinse it off—so it's best to rinse it thoroughly before cooking it. To rinse it, put the rice grains into the pot you'll be cooking them in. Add cool water to cover the rice, then swish the grains around with your fingers—the water will get cloudy. Carefully pour the cloudy water off the rice and repeat three or four times, until the water is clear when you pour it off.

KIMCHI PANCAKES

MAKES 6 small pancakes   TIME 30 minutes

2 cups kimchi, coarsely chopped, plus 2 tablespoons juice from the jar

½ cup all-purpose flour

½ cup rice flour

½ cup warm water

3 scallions (green parts only), cut into 1-inch pieces, plus more chopped scallions for garnish

1 tablespoon soy sauce

2 teaspoons sesame oil

¼ cup neutral-tasting oil (such as avocado oil), plus more as needed

Toasted sesame seeds, for garnish

Who knew that a scoop of spicy sour cabbage, mixed with some flour and fried up, would be such an addicting snack? These savory pancakes are best made with extra-ripe kimchi and paired with your favorite Korean dishes. I recommend the Bulgogi Japchac (page 107) and the Healing Miracle Seaweed Soup (page 85), or simply make enough for a tasty lunch. If serving as an appetizer, be sure to have the Soy Dipping Sauce (page 66) as well. This recipe can be doubled or tripled quite easily; just be sure to add more oil to the pan as you go.

1 In a large bowl, mix together the kimchi and its juice, all-purpose flour, rice flour, warm water, scallions, soy sauce, and sesame oil until you get a thick batter.

2 Heat a 10- or 12-inch cast-iron skillet over medium-high heat. When hot, add 2 tablespoons of the neutral oil, swirl the pan to coat the bottom with the oil, then use a spoon or spatula to spread about ¼ cup of the batter into a thin 4-inch round. Cook until nicely browned on the bottom,

3 to 4 minutes. Carefully flip the pancake, press down on it gently once or twice with a spatula, and cook until browned on the second side, another 2 to 3 minutes, adding an additional drizzle of oil to the pan as you turn if the pan seems dry.

3 Transfer the pancake to a plate lined with paper towels to soak up any excess oil. Repeat with the remaining batter. Serve hot, sprinkled with sesame seeds and chopped scallions.

CHEESY GARLIC BREAD

SERVES 6 to 8   **TIME** 40 minutes

1½ cups shredded whole-milk mozzarella cheese

¾ cup shredded sharp cheddar cheese (such as Tillamook)

¾ cup grated Parmesan cheese

1½ sticks (6 ounces) unsalted butter, at room temperature

5 to 8 garlic cloves, minced, to taste

1 (1-pound) loaf ciabatta or country bread

1 tablespoon finely chopped fresh flat-leaf parsley, for garnish

What's better than a side of gooey, melty cheesy garlic bread to accompany a hot soup, salad, or steak? This next-level garlic bread is extra cheesy and uses a mixture of cheeses to get you that stretchy, melty bite. Prepare the bread ahead of time, wrap it loosely in foil, and refrigerate it until ready to bake. It's best served piping hot out of the oven.

1 Preheat the oven to 375°F. Line a baking sheet with foil.

2 In a bowl, mix together the mozzarella, cheddar, Parmesan, butter, and garlic. Cut the loaf of bread in half horizontally (if using a baguette, you may need to cut the loaf in half crosswise first so it fits on the baking sheet) and arrange cut-sides up on the lined baking sheet.

Spread and smear the cheese and butter mixture onto the bread until it covers as much of the bread as possible.

3 Bake for 12 to 15 minutes, until the cheese is melty and golden brown, and the bread is crispy on the bottom. Remove from the oven and sprinkle with chopped parsley, then serve immediately.

PICKLED VEGETABLES

Slightly sweet, sour, and crunchy pickled vegetables are the ideal palate cleanser. The acid helps cut down the heaviness of a meaty meal while offering a refreshing break. Here are my essential pickled vegetables to pair with entrées.

PICKLED CARROTS AND DAIKON
MAKES about 2 cups   **TIME** 20 minutes, plus pickling time

Quick-pickled vegetables are great to have on hand for salads or snacking (and of course for the sliders made with Slow-Cooked Pork for Bánh Mì Sandwiches, page 166), but I especially love the color they add to Rockin' Beef Bowl (page 124). I like a roughly half-and-half mix of carrots and daikon, but use whatever combination you want!

1 medium carrot, cut into 2-inch matchsticks

1 daikon radish (about the same size as the carrot), peeled and cut into 2-inch matchsticks

¼ cup plus 1 tablespoon sugar

3 tablespoons kosher salt

1 cup warm water

1 cup distilled white vinegar

1   In a bowl, combine the carrot and daikon matchsticks, 1 tablespoon of the sugar, and 1 tablespoon of the salt and toss to blend. Let sit for 10 minutes to draw out the moisture. (After this period you should be able to bend and twist the carrot slices without breaking them.) Rinse off the vegetables and drain in a colander.

2   In a medium bowl, stir together the warm water and the remaining ¼ cup sugar and 2 tablespoons salt, stirring to dissolve. Add the white vinegar and the softened vegetables. Let sit for at least 1 hour to pickle, or refrigerate, covered, and let sit longer (preferably overnight or up to a week). Enjoy!

QUICK PICKLED RED ONIONS
MAKES about 2 cups   **TIME** 5 minutes, plus pickling time

I love the acidic crunch pickled onions add to each bite in a taco—but I make these for carnitas and carne asada, also. Pickled onions keep well in a sealed container in the fridge for a week.

1 red onion, thinly sliced

¼ cup sugar

2 tablespoons distilled white vinegar

1 tablespoon kosher salt

1 garlic clove (optional)

1 bay leaf (optional)

1 cup cold water

1   Place the onion in a bowl or mason jar. Add the sugar, white vinegar, salt, garlic (if using), bay leaf (if using), and cold water and mix well. Let it sit for at least 30 minutes to pickle.

2   Serve immediately, or store in the refrigerator, covered, up to 1 week.

KOREAN PICKLED JALAPEÑO AND RADISH

MAKES about 1 quart

TIME 15 minutes, plus at least 4 hours pickling time

1 cup soy sauce

1 cup distilled white vinegar

½ cup sugar

2 cups sliced Korean radish or daikon (peeled, quartered lengthwise, and cut into ⅛-inch-thick slices)

1 large jalapeño, cut into ⅛-inch-thick slices

¼ cup roughly chopped yellow onion

This is a Korean barbecue side dish staple, and it really livens up all of your taste buds. It has a kick of spiciness from the jalapeño and the overall flavor will be best if you make this recipe 2 days ahead of time. If you want less spicy pickles, remove the seeds from the jalapeño.

1 In a small saucepan, combine the soy sauce, white vinegar, and sugar. Bring to a boil over medium heat and cook, stirring occasionally, until the sugar dissolves. Remove the pan from the heat and let cool for about 10 minutes.

2 In a quart-size container, add the radish, jalapeño, and onion in alternating layers. Pour the soy sauce mixture into the container to completely submerge the veggies. Let it sit at room temperature for at least 4 hours, then enjoy, or cover and transfer to the refrigerator. Store, covered, up to 2 weeks.

QUICK SPICY PICKLED CUCUMBERS

MAKES about 2 cups   **TIME** 30 minutes, plus 1 hour pickling time

4 Persian (mini) cucumbers, cut into ½-inch-thick rounds

2 teaspoons kosher salt

2 teaspoons rice vinegar

1 teaspoon sesame oil

½ teaspoon toasted sesame seeds

1 garlic clove, minced

1 teaspoon sugar

1 teaspoon fish sauce

2 teaspoons gochugaru

These pickled cucumber medallions are seasoned with gochugaru (Korean chile flakes) to give them a spicy, bright red brine, but the chile can certainly be left out if you don't want any spice. They're the perfect accompaniment to just about any savory dish in this book!

1 In a medium bowl, mix the cucumbers with the salt until thoroughly coated. Transfer the cucumbers to a colander and let sit for 20 minutes. Rinse the cucumbers well (they should taste seasoned but not actually salty) and then pat them dry with paper towels.

2 In another medium bowl, combine the rice vinegar, sesame oil, sesame seeds, garlic, sugar, fish sauce, and gochugaru. Stir in the cucumbers (there won't be much liquid here), then cover and refrigerate for at least 1 hour (or up to 3 days) before serving. Enjoy!

DZUNG'S FAVORITE CONDIMENTS

FRIED SHALLOTS

MAKES about ⅓ cup   **TIME** 10 minutes

¼ cup avocado oil

1 large shallot, halved and thinly sliced

Although most Asian grocery stores sell premade fried shallots in a plastic container, they don't taste nearly as good as what you can make fresh in just a few minutes at home. The result is a crispy, crunchy topping that enhances Vietnamese dishes but is also pretty tempting as a stand-alone snack.

1 In a small saucepan, heat the oil over medium heat. When a slice of shallot sizzles immediately when added to the pan, add the shallots and cook until light golden brown, 2 to 4 minutes. (The shallots will continue to brown as they cool, so make sure you remove them before they're truly golden brown.)

2 Drain the shallots in a fine-mesh sieve set over a small bowl, then transfer the shallots to a plate lined with paper towels and spread them out to drain. Save the oil for Scallion Relish (below), or reuse for cooking. Serve the shallots immediately.

SCALLION RELISH

MAKES about ½ cup   **TIME** 5 minutes

3 tablespoons neutral-tasting oil (such as avocado oil)

3 scallions (green parts only), finely chopped

1 teaspoon kosher salt

1 teaspoon sugar

I can't remember a dish from my childhood that didn't have scallions as a garnish. I was never a huge fan then, but I've grown to like them. And whether I'm using raw scallions (I still prefer the green parts) or this warm, savory relish, I feel like they're part of most Vietnamese meals. Cooking the scallions for a moment in oil takes the edge off their sharp taste, and adding a pinch of salt and sugar gives them extra flavor. Drop the relish into a Vietnamese Grilled Pork Noodle Salad (page 110), smear it onto Grilled Salmon with Tamarind Dipping Sauce (page 132), or just keep it on hand as an extra flavor-boosting condiment!

1 In a small saucepan, heat the oil over medium heat. When the oil is hot, remove the pan from the heat and stir in the scallions, salt, and sugar. Stir until the salt and sugar dissolve, then serve, or set aside until ready to use.

2 The relish can be transferred to a small container and stored in the fridge for up to 1 week.

I saved the best and most interesting recipes for last: desserts! It just wouldn't be my cookbook if I didn't dedicate an entire chapter to my favorite things in life. I never miss dessert, and neither should you, so make sure your sweet tooth is on!

#MixMixMix
Your Favorite
Desserts

MEXICAN HOT CHOCOLATE POTS DE CRÈME

SERVES 4 or 6 **TIME** 45 minutes

7 ounces high-quality dark chocolate (70% cacao), finely chopped

2 cups half-and-half

2 tablespoons sugar

Pinch of kosher salt

3 large egg yolks

1 teaspoon ground cinnamon

1 teaspoon vanilla extract

Dash of cayenne pepper

A reimagined and enhanced Mexican hot chocolate is transformed into this recipe for chocolate pots de crème, or rich French-inspired custard pudding that you can easily make ahead. Garnish with whipped cream and extra chocolate shavings, for a fancy bistro touch.

1 Preheat the oven to 300°F. Set four 6-ounce or six 4-ounce ramekins in a roasting pan or 9 × 13-inch baking pan and set aside.

2 Put the chocolate in a heatproof medium bowl and set aside. In a medium saucepan, heat the half-and-half, sugar, and salt over medium-low heat until it comes to a simmer. Add the hot mixture to the bowl of chocolate and let it sit for about 3 minutes, stirring occasionally, until the chocolate has melted. Using an immersion blender, blend until smooth. (If you don't have one, cool the mixture for 5 minutes and transfer to a regular blender, then carefully blend with the top slightly open, so the heat can escape.)

3 In another bowl, whisk together the egg yolks, cinnamon, vanilla, and cayenne. Pour about 1 cup of the chocolate mixture into the eggs, whisking as you pour, then add the rest of the chocolate mixture and whisk to blend. Tap the bowl on the counter a few times to release any large air bubbles.

4 Place the pan with the ramekins near the oven. Divide the chocolate mixture evenly among the ramekins, filling each about three-quarters full, then transfer the pan to the middle oven rack. Carefully add warm water to the bottom of the pan until it comes about halfway up the sides of the ramekins. Slide the rack back in and bake for 20 to 25 minutes for smaller ramekins (or up to 30 minutes for larger ramekins), until the chocolate cream is set on the outsides but still a little jiggly in the centers. (Note that the actual time will depend on the temperature of the water when you add it, so use your judgment here.)

5 Remove the pan from the oven and carefully transfer the ramekins to a rack to cool for 20 minutes. Transfer the ramekins to the refrigerator to chill until firm, about 4 hours, or cover and chill overnight (or up to 3 days). Serve chilled.

STRAWBERRY-RASPBERRY-RHUBARB PIE

SERVES 8 **TIME** 2 hours 30 minutes

FOR THE CRUST

2 cups all-purpose flour, plus more for dusting

1 tablespoon granulated sugar

1 teaspoon kosher salt

1½ sticks (6 ounces) cold unsalted butter

⅓ to ½ cup ice water

FOR THE FRUIT FILLING

2 cups chopped rhubarb (about 3 large stalks)

2 cups chopped strawberries

2 cups (1 pint) raspberries

⅓ cup packed light brown sugar

3 tablespoons cornstarch

1 tablespoon lemon juice

1 teaspoon vanilla extract

½ teaspoon ground cinnamon

¼ teaspoon kosher salt

FOR THE CRUMBLE TOPPING

1¼ cups all-purpose flour

¾ cup packed dark brown sugar

6 tablespoons (¾ stick) unsalted butter, melted

½ teaspoon ground cinnamon

¼ teaspoon kosher salt

1 large egg whisked with 1 tablespoon water, for the egg wash

If you're not familiar with rhubarb, you're not alone. It wasn't until Nate mentioned his favorite pie was strawberry-rhubarb that I even thought to use it. So for his birthday one year, I decided to tackle this dessert. My testing left me thinking that there could be a stronger berry flavor, although the tartness from the buckwheat-related stalks really cut through. Raspberries were a solution that keeps all the colors popping. Also, my secret to a great pie crust is grating cold butter with a box grater, which means less physical work rolling the dough. This keeps the butter cold to ensure light, flaky layers in each bite. Let the pie cool before serving so the filling sets, and don't skip the vanilla ice cream!

1 **MAKE THE CRUST:** In a large bowl, whisk together the flour, granulated sugar, and salt. Using the large holes on a box grater, grate the butter and add it to the dry ingredients. Using both hands, work the butter into the dough between your thumbs and fingertips until all the pieces are pea-size or smaller. Slowly add ⅓ cup of the ice water, stirring the dough with a fork as you add it, and continue mixing until only a few dry spots remain at the bottom of the bowl. (If your dough needs more water, sprinkle it in about 1 tablespoon at a time, but don't exceed ½ cup water total. As soon as the dough forms a clump when you squeeze a handful of it together, you've added enough water.)

2 Transfer the dough to a large piece of plastic wrap. Wrap the plastic up and over the dough on all sides, forming a little package, then press the dough together to form a 1-inch-thick disc. The spots of butter you see will help create a flaky crust!

3 Place the dough in the fridge to rest for at least 30 minutes. (You can chill the dough overnight, too—just let it sit for 30 minutes on the counter, until pliable, before you roll it out.)

4 When you're ready to bake the pie, preheat the oven to 400°F.

5 **MAKE THE FRUIT FILLING:** In a large bowl, stir together the rhubarb, strawberries, raspberries, light brown sugar, cornstarch, lemon juice, vanilla, cinnamon, and salt. Set aside until ready to use.

6 **MAKE THE CRUMBLE TOPPING:** In a small bowl, stir together the flour, dark brown sugar, melted butter, cinnamon, and salt until evenly moist. Set aside.

7 Dust a clean work surface and a rolling pin with flour and roll out the dough to an approximately 11-inch round. Use the rolling pin to carefully transfer the dough to a 9-inch pie pan. Press the dough into the inside edges of the pan, and with scissors, trim the edges of the

(recipe continues)

dough so you have about ½ inch of dough hanging over on all sides. Fold the excess dough underneath itself, so you have a double layer of dough around the outside edge of the pan, then crimp the crust as desired. Brush the crimped edges with the egg wash.

8 Pour the fruit mixture into the crust, pat it down gently, then add the crumble mixture over the fruit and spread it out to cover the entire surface of the crumble.

9 Bake for 15 minutes, then reduce the oven temperature to 375°F and continue baking for 40 to 45 minutes, until the crust is golden brown and the filling is bubbling. (If the crust browns too quickly, you can cover the entire pie with foil.) Remove from the oven and let cool for at least 30 minutes to firm up the filling.

TIPS FOR BUZY LIVES Skip the Crust

If you want a stellar dessert in a little less time, just skip the crust and make a fruit crumble! Pile the filling mixture into a buttered 8 × 8-inch (or similar) glass or ceramic dish and top with the crumble topping. Bake at 375°F for 30 to 35 minutes, until browned on top and bubbling around the edges.

CHOCOLATE-CHERRY BLONDIES

MAKES 12 bars   **TIME** 30 minutes, plus cooling

8 tablespoons (1 stick) unsalted butter, at room temperature

¾ cup packed dark brown sugar

1 large egg

1 teaspoon vanilla extract

¼ teaspoon kosher salt

⅛ teaspoon baking soda

1 cup all-purpose flour

¾ cup dark chocolate chips (at least 60% cacao)

1 cup fresh cherries (about 18 cherries), pitted and quartered

This dessert may be the closest thing I make to a truly guilty pleasure. A chocolate chip cookie's flavor plus a brownie's texture with little gems of fruitiness, all with a scoop of ice cream? Is there a more complete dessert? I think not.

Craving it at a different time of year? Use raspberries if cherries are no longer in season.

1 Preheat the oven to 350°F. Line an 8 × 8-inch baking pan with a sheet of parchment paper so that the paper overhangs by about 2 inches on two of the sides.

2 In a bowl, with a hand mixer, beat the butter and brown sugar until light, about 2 minutes. (Or use a stand mixer fitted with the paddle attachment, beating on medium speed until light, about 1½ minutes.) Beat in the egg just until blended, pausing to scrape down the sides of the bowl if necessary, then beat in the vanilla, salt, and baking soda. Working by hand, fold in the flour with a soft spatula until mostly incorporated. Fold in the chocolate chips and cherries until no white spots of flour remain.

3 Spread the batter evenly in the prepared pan and bake for 20 to 22 minutes, until the middle is set and the edges are nice and golden brown. Cool the blondies for about 30 minutes in the pan, then, using the parchment paper as a sling, lift the blondies out of the pan and transfer to a large cutting board. Cut into 12 bars and enjoy! Store any uneaten bars at room temperature, covered with plastic or foil, up to 2 days.

TAKE IT FROM ME Pitting Cherries

If you don't have a cherry pitter, here's a DIY version: Poke the thicker end of a chopstick or a strong metal straw into the stem end of the cherry, push it through, and voilà! Out comes the pit. Super easy!

GINGER-CARDAMOM LEMON BARS

MAKES 12 bars **TIME** 50 minutes, plus cooling time

Lemon bars are universally beloved, and in California, where citrus is available year-round, I make some of my best batches during the holiday season. The sunny and tart combo, with a hint of ginger and tingling spices, makes the party-size batch perfect for a get-together, anytime.

FOR THE CRUST

1¼ cups all-purpose flour

8 tablespoons (1 stick) unsalted butter, at room temperature, cut into ½-inch pieces

½ cup granulated sugar

½ teaspoon kosher salt

½ teaspoon ground cardamom

FOR THE FILLING

4 large eggs

1 cup granulated sugar

1 teaspoon ground ginger

¼ teaspoon kosher salt

Grated zest of 1 lemon

½ cup lemon juice (4 to 5 lemons)

¼ cup whole milk

¼ cup all-purpose flour

Powdered sugar, for serving

1 Preheat the oven to 350°F.

2 **MAKE THE CRUST:** In a food processor, pulse together the flour, butter, granulated sugar, salt, and cardamom to blend, then whirl until the ingredients are evenly moist and no small butter pieces are visible, about 30 seconds.

3 Transfer the dough to a 9-inch square baking dish and pat it down into an even layer. Bake for 15 to 18 minutes, until lightly golden brown. Remove from the oven and cool for 10 minutes. (Leave the oven on.)

4 **MEANWHILE, MAKE THE FILLING:** In a bowl, whisk together the eggs, granulated sugar, ginger, and salt until well blended. Add the lemon zest, lemon juice, and milk and whisk again to combine. Add the flour and whisk until the batter is smooth.

5 Pour the filling over the warm crust, return to the oven, and bake for 18 to 20 minutes, until the filling is set in the center and just beginning to brown at the edges.

6 Let the bars cool at room temperature for 1 hour (or let cool completely). Sift a thin layer of powdered sugar over the filling, run a small knife around the edge, cut into 12 bars, and serve. Store any uneaten bars covered in the refrigerator, up to 3 days, and bring to room temperature before serving.

EARL GREY TART *with* BLOOD ORANGES AND POMEGRANATE

SERVES 6 to 8 **TIME** 2 hours, plus chilling time

FOR THE PASTRY CREAM

2 cups whole milk

1 teaspoon vanilla extract

½ teaspoon finely ground Earl Grey tea (from a bag)

2 large eggs

½ cup sugar

3 tablespoons cornstarch

¼ teaspoon kosher salt

3 tablespoons unsalted butter, cut into small cubes

FOR THE DOUGH

8 tablespoons (1 stick) unsalted butter, melted

2 tablespoons sugar

¼ teaspoon kosher salt

1⅓ cups all-purpose flour

FOR SERVING

2 blood oranges

⅓ cup pomegranate seeds

This eye-popping, colorful tart is infused with the distinct notes of Earl Grey tea, enhanced by a blood orange sweetness, and accented by ruby pomegranate bursts. When making the pastry cream, be sure to use bagged tea (I'd suggest Twinings or Republic of Tea brands) and not the loose-leaf kind, which will give your pastry cream an unpleasant texture. Bake and fill the tart up to a day ahead of time, and for the freshest look, add the fruits right before serving—you can peel the oranges and then slice them, as directed below, or leave the peel on and slice them as thin as possible for a more dramatic look. If you can't find blood oranges in season, substitute with navel oranges or Cara Caras, which have more of a pinkish hue.

1 **MAKE THE PASTRY CREAM:** In a small saucepan, combine the milk, vanilla, and tea. Place the pan over medium heat and cook, stirring occasionally, until the mixture begins to steam.

2 Meanwhile, in a bowl, whisk together the eggs, sugar, cornstarch, and salt until smooth.

3 Add about ½ cup of the warmed milk to the egg mixture, whisking as you pour, then repeat, adding another ½ cup or so of the milk. (You're bringing the eggs up to temperature slowly here.) Then, pour the warmed egg mixture into the saucepan with the rest of the milk and place over medium heat. Cook, whisking frequently, until the mixture starts to steam again, then whisk constantly until the mixture begins to thicken. While whisking, add the butter, about 1 tablespoon at a time, mixing until the cream is glossy and thick. Immediately transfer the cream to a bowl and cover directly with plastic wrap, so the plastic touches the cream. Let the cream cool for about 10 minutes on the counter, then refrigerate for 1 hour, or until room temperature or colder.

4 **MEANWHILE, MAKE THE DOUGH:** In a bowl, whisk together the melted butter, sugar, and salt. Add the flour and stir with a spoon until the dough is well combined, then knead the dough by hand a few times in the bowl to make sure all the flour is combined.

5 Crumble the mixture evenly across the bottom of a 9-inch round or a 14 × 4-inch rectangular tart pan with a removable bottom (if you don't have one with a removable bottom, simply line a tart pan or 9 × 9-inch pan with a strip of parchment paper, so you can use the paper as a sling for removing the tart when it's finished). Using your hands, press the dough into a thin, even layer along the bottom and up

(recipe continues)

the sides of the pan. With a fork, prick the dough all over the bottom of the pan. Cover and chill the tart shell in the freezer for at least 10 minutes, or in the fridge for at least 1 hour, or up to 24 hours.

6 Preheat the oven to 350°F.

7 Place the tart shell on a baking sheet and bake for 18 to 20 minutes, until golden brown. Transfer the crust to a cooling rack and let cool to room temperature.

8 Once the pastry cream and crust have both cooled completely, pour the pastry cream into the crust and smooth it out with an offset spatula or a dull knife, so it fills the crust all the way to the edges. Chill the tart for at least 4 hours, or until the cream has set.

9 Before serving, remove the tart from the pan and transfer it to a serving plate. Cut the peel and any white pith off the blood oranges and cut them into slices or segments, removing any seeds as you go. Arrange the oranges and pomegranate seeds however you'd like. (Be artful and creative here! I like adding various sizes of blood orange slices first and filling in the gaps with the pomegranate seeds. Just make sure to cover the pastry cream completely.) The tart is at its prettiest served immediately, but you could also chill it another few hours before serving.

LYCHEE-ROSE NO-BAKE CHEESECAKES

MAKES 12 mini cheesecakes
TIME 45 minutes, plus chilling and cooling time

24 Biscoff cookies

4 tablespoons (½ stick) unsalted butter, melted

1½ cups lychee fruit (about 24 lychees, from a 20-ounce can), plus ¼ cup lychee syrup, chilled

2 tablespoons granulated sugar

1 (¼-ounce) envelope unflavored gelatin

12 ounces (1½ blocks) cream cheese, at room temperature

½ cup powdered sugar

1 cup plain whole-milk Greek yogurt

2 tablespoons lime juice

1 teaspoon vanilla extract

½ teaspoon rose water

Pinch of kosher salt

1 cup heavy cream

12 strawberries, sliced

Edible rose petals, for garnish

I love no-bake cheesecakes because they take less effort to make than your traditional cheesecake, and I can lighten them up by using Greek yogurt. Here, I infuse the cheesecake with fresh bits of tropical flavor from the lychee and pair it with light and subtle floral notes from the rose to give this no-bake treat a gourmet flare.

If you can't locate Biscoff cookies, graham crackers or gingersnaps will do—you'll need about 1½ cups of crumbs. (You can purchase premade graham cracker crumbs, too.) And keep any leftover crust to sprinkle over yogurt or for the Key Lime Pie Chia Puddings (page 56)!

You'll need either twelve 4-ounce mason jars or a nonstick mini cheesecake mold pan here.

1 In a food processor or blender, whirl the cookies until evenly sandy. Add the melted butter, and pulse until all the crumbs are moist and the mixture begins to clump together. Transfer 1 heaping tablespoon to each of twelve 4-ounce mason jars (or divide it evenly among 12 cavities of a mini cheesecake mold) and tamp the crust firmly into an even layer that covers the entire bottom of the jars. (A tiny cup, the tamp from a Vietnamese coffee filter, or the blunt end of a lemon reamer all work well.)

2 In a clean food processor or blender, puree the lychees until almost smooth. Pour the blended fruit into a saucepan, add 1 tablespoon of the granulated sugar, and bring to a boil over medium heat. Cook at a hard simmer until the liquid has reduced and the mixture has thickened to about the consistency of applesauce, 5 to

10 minutes. Transfer the puree to a bowl and put aside to cool completely, about 30 minutes.

3 In a small microwave-safe bowl, whisk together the gelatin and the lychee syrup until smooth, then set it aside and let it thicken as it swells up. (This is called "blooming" the gelatin.) Once it has fully bloomed, microwave the gelatin for 20 seconds, just until it becomes clear and fully liquefied again. (If it's not quite clear, microwave again at 5-second increments.) Set aside.

4 In a large bowl, with a hand mixer, whip the cream cheese with the powdered sugar until fluffy and smooth, about 2 minutes. (Or use a stand mixer fitted with the paddle attachment, whipping on medium-high speed for about 1 minute.) Add the yogurt, lime juice, vanilla, rose water, and salt. Mix again for another minute (or just about 30 seconds with the stand mixer), until fluffy and combined. Add

(recipe continues)

the liquefied gelatin mixture and the cooled lychee puree and mix everything together until smooth, scraping the sides and bottom of the bowl as necessary to make sure everything is incorporated. The mixture will begin to thicken almost immediately.

5 Fill each of the mason jars (or the cheesecake molds) about two-thirds of the way with the cheesecake mixture. Refrigerate for at least 4 hours or up to 48 hours.

6 Before serving, whip the heavy cream with the remaining 1 tablespoon sugar (with the hand mixer, about 2 minutes, or 1 to 2 minutes in a stand mixer fitted with the whisk attachment), until medium peaks form. Serve the cheesecakes in their mason jars (or pop the cheesecakes out of their molds and transfer them to a plate) topped with whipped cream, sliced strawberries, and a few rose petals, and enjoy!

COCONUT-MANGO RICE PUDDING

SERVES 4 **TIME** 45 minutes

FOR THE RICE PUDDING

½ cup Arborio rice

¼ cup small-size tapioca pearls

1 (13.5-ounce) can full-fat coconut milk

¼ cup sugar

½ teaspoon vanilla extract

Pinch of kosher salt

FOR THE MANGO SAUCE

2 cups peeled and roughly chopped fresh mango (such as Champagne or Keitt) or frozen mango chunks

1 tablespoon honey

Juice of ½ lime

1 mango, diced, for serving

Within Vietnamese cuisine there's a category of desserts called *chè*, which consists of sweet drinks, soups, and puddings. They're enjoyed hot or cold, sweet or sometimes savory, and typically combined with beans, taro, or tapioca. They can also be topped with a sugary coconut cream sauce. I had many *chè* growing up but always thought they could be fruitier. Here I've mixed rice and tapioca together and freshened them up with a light tropical glaze. (Note that you're looking for the small tapioca beads used for desserts, not the larger boba-size pearls used for drinks.) Use any mango variety you'd like here; I recommend Champagne (Ataulfo) or Keitt mangoes because they're sweeter.

1 MAKE THE RICE PUDDING: In a small saucepan, combine the rice, tapioca pearls, coconut milk, sugar, vanilla, and kosher salt. Stir in 2¼ cups water and bring the mixture to a boil over medium-high heat, stirring to help the sugar dissolve. When it boils, reduce the heat and cook at a bare simmer, stirring frequently so the rice does not stick to the bottom of the pot, until the rice and tapioca pearls soak up the liquid and are creamy, chewy, and soft, 45 to 50 minutes. Remove from the heat and set aside.

2 MEANWHILE, MAKE THE MANGO SAUCE: In a saucepan, combine the mango, honey, lime juice, and ½ cup water. (If you're using frozen mango, increase the water to ¾ cup.) Bring the liquid to a boil, reduce the heat to low, and simmer until the mangoes are soft and the water is almost gone, about 10 minutes (or 15 minutes for frozen mango). Mash the mangoes into a puree (or use an immersion blender to make a smoother sauce).

3 Serve the rice pudding in small bowls or ramekins, topped with the mango sauce and fresh mangos. Serve immediately.

MATCHA CHOCOLATE LAVA CAKES

MAKES 4 cakes   **TIME** 1 hour 15 minutes

FOR THE MATCHA GANACHE

½ cup white chocolate chips

1 tablespoon coconut oil, melted

1½ teaspoons matcha powder

FOR THE CAKES

Melted butter and all-purpose flour, for the ramekins

8 tablespoons (1 stick) unsalted butter

4 ounces dark chocolate (at least 60% cacao), chopped

1 tablespoon all-purpose flour

2 large eggs

2 large egg yolks

3 tablespoons sugar

Matcha powder, for serving

Carefully carving into a delicate chocolate cake to have a sweet lava ooze forth is a breathtaking dessert moment, and now you can make this magic in your own kitchen! This matcha lava cake is a balance of buttery white chocolate, rich dark cocoa, and bitter matcha earthiness, and it's with less than 30 minutes of actual work.

See Making Matcha (page 33) for more information on matcha powder. When you make the ganache, consider doubling the recipes so you have enough to make Matcha White Hot Chocolate (page 33)!

1 Preheat the oven to 450°F.

2 **MAKE THE MATCHA GANACHE:** Fill a small saucepan with about an inch of water. Set a heatproof bowl over the pan, making sure the bottom of the bowl doesn't touch the water, and bring the water to a simmer over medium-high heat. Add the white chocolate chips, coconut oil, and matcha powder to the bowl and cook, stirring, until the mixture is melted and smooth. Remove the bowl from the pan immediately, then divide the mixture among four spaces in a 1¼-inch-square silicone ice cube tray, taking care to fill each space all the way to the top. Freeze until the cubes can be easily removed in one piece, about 45 minutes.

3 **MEANWHILE, MAKE THE CAKES:** Brush the insides of four 4-ounce ramekins with melted butter, then dust lightly with flour and tap to remove any excess flour. Arrange the ramekins on a baking sheet.

4 Set another heatproof bowl over a small saucepan of simmering water and melt the butter. Add the dark chocolate and stir until smooth, then remove the bowl from the pan.

5 In another bowl, with a hand mixer, beat the whole eggs, egg yolks, and sugar on high speed until fluffy and a shade lighter in color, a minute or two. (Or use a stand mixer fitted with the whisk attachment, whisking on medium-high speed for about 1 minute.) Pour the egg mixture into the chocolate mixture, add the flour, and mix gently until no streaks remain.

6 Fill each ramekin with ¼ cup of the cake batter, then plop 1 cube of the ganache filling into the center of each. Divide the remaining cake batter among the ramekins, taking care to cover the filling completely. Bake the cakes for 7 to 9 minutes, until puffed but still a little shiny in the center.

7 When the cakes are done, transfer them to a cooling rack and let cool for 10 minutes. To serve, invert each ramekin onto a dessert plate, then gently remove the ramekin, tapping the sides as necessary to encourage the cake to pop out. Dust the cake with matcha and serve immediately.

MOM'S FAMOUS FLAN

SERVES 6 to 8   **TIME** 1 hour, plus cooling and chilling time

1½ cups sugar

3½ cups whole milk

5 large eggs

4 large egg yolks

2 tablespoons Kahlúa liqueur

1 teaspoon vanilla extract

My mom has become known for her Vietnamese-style flan because over the years it's appeared at most family birthdays, holidays, ancestor remembrance days . . . and probably many other occasions. It's rooted deep in my family's history. Traditionally made by her father, she grew up with it in Vietnam, and it has since become a celebration of home whenever she felt nostalgic. The Kahlúa in this recipe is my mom's "Honeysuckle" twist. Ignore any perceptions you may have about flan being difficult to make; this golden custard dessert is actually quite simple.

1 Position a rack in the center of the oven and preheat the oven to 325°F.

2 In a medium saucepan, combine ¾ cup of the sugar and ¼ cup water. Don't stir it, but place it over medium-high heat and let the sugar melt. Continue cooking, undisturbed, until the sugar turns a deep amber or reads 340° to 350°F on an instant-read candy thermometer. Remove the pan from the heat and immediately pour the caramel into an 8-inch cake pan, turning the pan carefully to spread it into an even layer on the entire bottom of the pan. Set aside.

3 In a medium saucepan, heat the milk over medium heat until it begins to steam. While the milk warms, in a bowl, whisk together the whole eggs, egg yolks, and the remaining ¾ cup sugar until evenly blended but not foamy. Once the milk is steaming, add about ½ cup of the milk to the egg mixture, whisking as you add it to warm the eggs up a touch. While whisking, slowly add the rest of the milk to the bowl—but don't whisk so hard that you create foam. Stir in the

Kahlúa and vanilla. Pour the mixture through a fine-mesh sieve into the prepared caramel cake pan.

4 Place the cake pan in a 9 × 9-inch baking pan (or something else large enough to comfortably hold the cake pan) and fill the bottom of the baking pan with warm water until the water comes halfway up the side of the cake pan. Bake on the middle rack for 45 to 50 minutes, until the edges are just set. (The entire thing should wobble in one piece, rather than just in the center.)

5 Remove the pans from the oven, transfer the cake pan to a cooling rack, and let cool completely. Once cool, transfer the flan to the refrigerator and chill for at least 4 hours or up to 24 hours. (If you're waiting a day to serve it, cover the pan with plastic wrap.)

6 When ready to serve, gently separate the flan from the edges of the pan with a thin knife and place a plate on top of the cake pan. Flip both over and lift the cake pan off the flan. Cut the flan into wedges and serve, drizzled with any extra caramel from the pan on top.

DZUNG AND NATE'S FAVORITE BANANA CAKE

SERVES 10 to 12   **TIME** 1 hour 30 minutes, plus cooling and chilling time

FOR THE CAKE

Butter and flour, for the pans

2½ cups all-purpose flour

1 teaspoon baking powder

½ teaspoon baking soda

1 teaspoon kosher salt

3 large very ripe bananas

2 sticks (8 ounces) unsalted butter, at room temperature

1 cup granulated sugar

½ cup packed dark brown sugar

2 large eggs

½ cup plain whole-milk Greek yogurt

2 teaspoons vanilla extract

FOR THE FROSTING

4 cups powdered sugar

12 ounces (1½ blocks) cream cheese, at room temperature

4 tablespoons (½ stick) unsalted butter, at room temperature

2 teaspoons vanilla extract

1 teaspoon kosher salt

Our wedding cake was a gorgeous banana cake with cream cheese frosting that sat atop an abundant outdoor dessert bar. And each year we celebrate our anniversary with a similar, family-size one. I've tinkered with the recipe over the years, taking down the sweetness of the frosting, but our fondness for its velvety lusciousness only grows. And it usually doubles as my birthday breakfast because that's the very next day!

1 **MAKE THE CAKE:** Preheat the oven to 350°F. Butter and flour the bottoms and sides of two 8- or 9-inch round cake pans. Line the bottoms with rounds of parchment paper.

2 In a bowl, whisk together the flour, baking powder, baking soda, and salt. In another bowl, mash the bananas until soft but still a bit chunky. Set both bowls aside.

3 In a stand mixer fitted with the paddle attachment (or using a hand mixer), whip the butter on medium-high speed until soft, about 2 minutes. Add the granulated and dark brown sugars and continue mixing until the mixture is pale and fluffy, another 3 to 4 minutes. Scrape down the sides and bottom of the bowl. With the mixer on low speed, add the eggs one at a time, mixing until incorporated after each addition and scraping down the sides as needed. Add the yogurt and vanilla and mix again on low speed until combined.

4 Add the bananas and the flour mixture in two additions on low speed, mixing briefly between additions and alternating the two, starting with the bananas and ending with the flour mixture, mixing until most of the flour is incorporated. Remove the bowl from the mixer and gently fold in any last bits of flour by hand—the batter will be quite thick.

5 Scrape the batter into the prepared pans, smooth each into an even layer with an offset spatula or the back of a spoon, and bake for 28 to 30 minutes (for 8-inch cakes) or 25 to 28 minutes (for 9-inch cakes), until the cakes are golden brown around the edges and cooked through and a toothpick inserted in the center comes out clean. (You can rotate the pans after about 20 minutes if they seem to be browning unevenly.) Remove from the oven and let them cool completely in the pans (about 3 hours).

6 WHEN THE CAKES ARE COOL, MAKE THE FROSTING: In a stand mixer fitted with the paddle attachment (or using a hand mixer), beat together the powdered sugar, cream cheese, butter, vanilla, and salt on low speed until combined, starting with a few quick on-off pulses to prevent the sugar from jumping out of the bowl. Once combined, increase the speed to medium-high and beat until the frosting is very light and fluffy, about 3 minutes.

7 ASSEMBLE THE CAKE: If necessary, use a long serrated knife to trim the domed tops off the cake layers. Place one layer bottom-side down on a platter or cake stand. Spread a generous ½ cup of the frosting on top, then add the second layer, bottom-side up. (This keeps the top of the cake flat.) Use another generous ½ cup of the frosting to fill in the gap between the cakes and spread a thin layer of frosting, known as a crumb coat, over the entire cake. Refrigerate the cake for about 1 hour, until the crumb coat is firm.

8 Finish frosting the cake with the remaining frosting (you may not use all of it) and refrigerate again for at least 30 minutes, or up to 24 hours, before serving. (If you refrigerate the cake for more than 1 hour, let it come to room temperature for about 1 hour before serving.) Enjoy!

VANILLA-BOURBON CREAM PUFFS

MAKES 12 large or 16 smaller puffs   TIME 50 minutes, plus cooling time

FOR THE CREAM PUFFS

6 tablespoons (¾ stick) unsalted butter

1 teaspoon granulated sugar

Pinch of salt

1 cup all-purpose flour

4 large eggs

FOR THE VANILLA-BOURBON WHIPPED CREAM

1 teaspoon unflavored gelatin

1 tablespoon cold water

1 cup heavy cream, well chilled

⅓ cup powdered sugar

1 tablespoon bourbon

1 teaspoon vanilla extract

The crunchy shell and creamy filling of a cream puff are an irresistible tandem that's hard to match. These bourbon-infused morsels are lightly balanced with sweetness, an ideal holiday treat or morning coffee pastry. Because the whipped cream is stabilized with gelatin, the cream firms up a bit after you make them, so they stay perky for a party. But they're still best served chilled.

For an elegant presentation, instead of forming sandwiches, leave the cream puffs whole and pipe the filling with a star tip into the bottom of each cream puff.

1 Preheat the oven to 425°F. Line a baking sheet with parchment paper and set aside. Chill a metal bowl (or the work bowl of a stand mixer) for whipping the cream.

2 FIRST, MAKE THE CREAM PUFFS: In a medium saucepan, combine the butter, granulated sugar, salt, and 1 cup water. Bring the mixture to a boil over medium-high heat. Once the butter has fully melted, remove the pan from the heat and add the flour all at once. Using a wooden spoon, stir the mixture vigorously until the dough clumps into a ball and cleans the sides of the pan.

3 Then add the eggs one at a time, mixing vigorously with a wooden spoon until the mixture is thick and homogenous and no longer slippery after each addition.

4 Next, transfer the dough to a piping bag fitted with a round tip (or into a large zip-top bag with one corner cut off) and pipe the dough onto the prepared baking sheet into something that looks like kisses the size of golf balls. (You can make 12 or 16 puffs, depending on how big you want them to be, but just make sure

to space them evenly on the baking sheet, as they will expand in the oven.) Using wet fingers, pat down any spikes that formed on the top of your puffs when you piped them.

5 Transfer the baking sheet to the oven and bake for 25 to 30 minutes (less for smaller puffs, more for larger ones), until the pastry has puffed up and is a lovely golden brown. Try not to open the oven during baking, as it could flatten the puffs during the baking process. Remove the puffs from the oven and transfer them to a rack to cool, about 30 minutes.

6 WHEN THE PUFFS ARE COOL, MAKE THE VANILLA-BOURBON WHIPPED CREAM: In a small microwave-safe bowl, whisk together the gelatin and cold water until smooth, then set it aside and let it thicken until it swells up. (This is called "blooming" the gelatin.) Once it has fully bloomed, microwave the gelatin for 20 seconds, just until it becomes clear and fully liquefied again. (If it's not quite clear, microwave again in 5-second increments.) Set aside.

7 In the chilled bowl, whisk together the chilled cream, powdered sugar, bourbon, and vanilla until soft peaks form, 1 to 2 minutes. Slowly add the gelatin mixture and continue whisking until incorporated. (Tip: If the gelatin begins to harden before you incorporate it into the whipping cream, microwave it for a few seconds until it liquefies again. Swirl to let it cool a bit and then proceed.)

Continue whipping until stiff peaks form, another minute or so—you want it to be stable but still smooth.

8 Cut the cooled cream puffs in half horizontally. Add a heaping tablespoon or two of the cream to the bottom half of each pastry, replace the tops, and chill until ready to serve, up to 6 hours. Dust with powdered sugar and enjoy!

TIPS FOR BUZY LIVE We All Scream!

Don't limit yourself to whipped cream for filling the cream puffs. You could also fill them with the Earl Grey pastry cream (from the Earl Grey Tart with Blood Oranges and Pomegranate, page 213); on a hot day, stuff them with your favorite ice cream—coffee, chocolate, or strawberry flavors would all be lovely.

MENU IDEAS

BREAKFAST IN BED

Turn Up the Beet Drink
(page 38)

Mushroom and Kale Savory
Oatmeal (page 43)

Apricot-Walnut-Cardamom
Granola Yogurt Cups
(page 50)

BRUNCH WITH FRIENDS

Rose Milk Tea (page 34)

Orange-Pistachio French Toast
(page 68)

Matcha-Almond Breakfast Loaf
(page 71)

Crepes with Goat Cheese–
Scrambled Eggs (page 62)

Ginger-Cardamom Lemon Bars
(page 210)

NO-STRESS HOLIDAY DINNER

Butternut Squash Soup
(page 89)

Pressure Cooker Prime Rib
(page 175)

Tomatoes Provençale
(page 184)

Crispy Brussels Sprouts with
Chile-Lime-Garlic Sauce
(page 191)

Tartiflette (page 188)

Vanilla-Bourbon Cream Puffs
(page 226)

MOVIE NIGHT ON THE COUCH

Kimchi Mac and Cheese
(page 115)

Truffled Mushroom Flatbread
Pizza (page 144)

Chocolate-Cherry Blondies
(page 209)

Vanilla-Lavender Steamed Milk
(page 30)

LIGHT SUMMER DINNER
PARTY

Chile-Lime Street Fruit Salad
(page 78)

Squash Tacos with Cilantro-
Lime Slaw (page 140)

Salt and Pepper Shrimp (Tom
Rang Muoi) (page 139)

Mexican Hot Chocolate Pots de
Crème (page 205)

KOREAN BBQ AT HOME

Korean Pickled Jalapeño and
Radish (page 200)

Quick Spicy Pickled Cucumbers
(page 200)

Kimchi Pancakes (page 194)

Bulgogi Japchae (page 107)

Pan-Seared Steak with
Ssamjang Glaze (page 135)

TASTE OF VIETNAM DINNER

Vietnamese Pan-Fried Rice
Cakes (Bánh Bột Chiên)
(page 65)

Vietnamese Vegetarian
Tamarind Soup (Canh Chua
Chay) (page 97)

Vietnamese Caramelized Fish
(Ca Kho To) (page 147)

Coconut-Mango Rice Pudding
(page 219)

BETTER THAN TAKEOUT NIGHT

Hot and Sour Soup (page 98)

Chicken Chow Mein (page 109)

Thai Shrimp-Fried Rice
(page 126)

Veggie Mu Shu (page 148)

White Rice (page 192)

COZY NIGHT IN

Nate's Turkey Meatballs
(page 160)

Cheesy Garlic Bread (page 197)

Matcha Chocolate Lava Cakes
(page 220)

SPRING SOIREE OR EASTER
FEAST

Spring Farro and Veggie Salad
(page 75)

Quino Pilaf with Curry-Miso
Dressing (page 179)

Fast or Slow Lambchetta
(page 170)

Earl Grey Tart with Blood
Oranges and Pomegranate
(page 213)

YOU SAID IT!

"Thanks for sharing your family and life with us! And yes, fish sauce is the Vietnamese secret weapon for everything." —Doodah Gurl

"I wish you had a typed version of your recipes!" —Michelle Van

"Dzung, I just love love love everything about your videos and about you! You feel like a friend after watching all your videos . . . thanks for the good stuff."
—Nicky Louis

"Interesting. I've only ever thought of flavoring lattes or coffees with flavored syrup. I'm going to try orange zest!" —Natalie

"My bff and I just made the egg custard coffee and it was amazing! Now I'm already craving another one! Thank you!!!!" —ninaslice

"I just started drinking this remedy last night and this is not only delicious but OMG it has made me feel so much better!!!!" —Liza C

"Savory oats are the best! I usually use chicken or veggie broth instead of water to ramp up the flavor."
—Angela Kao

"I just tried your tomato soup and this is the best thing I have ever done. It really tastes perfect and it's not too heavy on the stomach."
—Amandine Da Silva

"I really appreciate that you make quick easy but still *pretty* authentic versions of these dishes!! As a college student that lives far away from home and misses their mothers cooking and loves cooking but has little time, this is great!"
—Jayce Nguyen

"This is my favorite takeout order. Good to know how easy it is to make at home too plus those egg ribbons are fun to watch."
—Perspective Portions

"Slivers of unripe mangos, apples, and pineapples are great to add sweetness to the spring rolls as well!" —Britney Le

"Omg! My mom taught me how to measure water/liquid for rice the same way with the index finger trick! She learned from her mom also."
—Janice Wang

THANK-YOUS

To my *Honeysuckle* family, the "Buzybeez": You asked for years for a place to find my written recipes. It's been a journey to get here, but this book is for you. It's a #mixmixmix of recipes that you loved on my channel and new ones that I hope will inspire more cooking and experimenting in your kitchens. I have loved sharing my stories week after week with you and have learned so much from you and the types of food you enjoy. I've taken notes and tweaked some old favorites with your comments in mind. I truly would not be here if it weren't for your support and kindness to help build this community through social media. This is the extension of our Internet community that I hope will be a valuable reference in your home kitchen! I can't wait to see what you whip up.

Alix, Denise, and the DBA team: I can't think of a better team to work with day in and day out. Alix, thank you for believing in me, for pushing me to create this book, and for supporting my dreams of making this and *Honeysuckle* happen. Your daily support of our business has taken us to new levels. You all have changed our lives, and we wouldn't be here if it weren't for you.

Anna Worrall, I wasn't even thinking of writing a book until you came along and convinced me that now is the time to do this. This beautiful book baby was born because of you. Thank you for being there every single step of the way and for making this daunting process somewhat manageable. You have such a calm way of explaining things to me and you really helped me navigate my way through this completely new territory.

Jess Thomson, we hit it off immediately when this book relationship was born. Your way with words transformed my gibberish. I love that you understand my taste buds and my thoughts, and you helped me through endless indecisions. I hope this process gave you new appreciation for Vietnamese and Asian food!

To everyone at Rodale: Dervla Kelly, Stephanie Huntwork, Katherine Leak, Joyce Wong, Kelli Tokos, and Nick Patton, plus the marketing team: Christina Foxley, Odette Fleming, Tammy Blake, and Leilani Zee.

You have been a dream to work with, from recipe conception to design of this book; it has been such a collaborative process. Thank you for your support and confidence in me and the *Honeysuckle* brand. I'm still pinching myself that this book is really happening!

Eva Kolenko, the photography in this book is pure art, and it's all because of you, your vision, and your unique style. Somehow you and Ryan managed to make my ugly dining table look beautiful! I knew I was in good hands when you sent me that first text with the Overnight Thai Tea photo, and then each photo just got better and better, exceeding my expectations in the most delightful way. You are truly an artist and such a joy to work with. I hope we get the opportunity to work together again!

Ryan Reineck, you made each and every recipe look so beautiful and stylish. The art direction for each shot really brought the food to life and told my story. I am blown away by your keen eye for detail. Also, Sip-n-Giggle Saturday was the best, and I will always think of you when someone tells me look away and laugh. Ah-hahaha . . . :)

Natalie Drobny and Liza Myers: You worked tirelessly to re-create the recipes and took such great care in making sure some unfamiliar dishes were exactly as they should be. Thank you for being so meticulous. Natalie, I appreciated your feedback on the recipes, and your recommendation to add gochujang in the kimchi mac and cheese made it complete.

Rule & Level Studios (Claire Mack and David Gantz): Thank you for hosting the photo shoot. Your studio is an absolute dream. I admired each and every square foot of the space and all of the beautiful props on display that we had the opportunity to use. Claire, I couldn't believe you created those additional pink pieces for us to use. Dave, you checked on us every day and made sure we had everything we needed. Your hospitality was so incredibly appreciated.

To my parents. Mom and Dad, thank you for introducing me to delicious food at such a young age, making me sit at the dinner table well after everyone was done, and encouraging me to explore food so I wouldn't become a picky eater. Tough love worked. LOL! Daddy, I miss you so much and wish you were here to see this book in person, but I know you are looking down on me and rooting me on during this whole process. You took me to buy the first piece of meat to make the beef roulade we saw someone make on PBS and have supported this passion from day one. Momma, your critical taste buds helped me perfect all the Vietnamese recipes in this book. Your flan recipe will live on forever, and I'm so glad we'll be able to pass it down for generations to come. I hope both you and Daddy are proud of how far I've come!

Tram, you've pretty much helped me through everything in life, but more specifically thanks for responding to my endless texts, talking to me through mental recipe blocks and meltdowns, for helping me remember some parts of our childhood so I could retell them here, and for giving your honest opinion of my recipes, even if my recipe sucked. I can always count on you to give it to me straight. Thank you for flying to LA to be a part of this book. It meant so much to me. Love you, sis!

Gina and UJ, you were our incubator and our support team as we dreamed and started pursuing this crazy YouTube career. Thank you for letting us take over your kitchen and house every Sunday for years until we were able to use our own space to film. *Honeysuckle* was truly born in your kitchen. You were always our biggest cheerleaders for everything in life, and we love you so much.

Barb, I consider myself *so* lucky to have had that second chance to work with you at *Sunset* after the Chase program got canceled. You recognized how special *Honeysuckle* was even before social media became what it is today. You are my mentor and second mom. You and Jeff treat Nate, then Ollie, and the kids like your family, and we love you both so much for that. I hope to one day be as great of a leader, mom, and female role model as you. Thank you for your advice and thoughtful feedback throughout this book-writing process—your opinion, especially, was invaluable.

Maly, you helped me learn how to bake for reals. I remember when we decided to have a baking day and I brought a bunch of box mixes and you put your foot down and said no, we are baking from scratch. From that day on, I was determined to work on this skill—all thanks to you.

To Mark, Nate's dad, Khiet, and the rest of my dear friends and family: Your support has been so appreciated. While most people would enjoy getting free food or have someone cook for them, I forced you to eat my food and asked for your brutal and honest opinion. I made you look at potential covers and continued to harass you through texts and ask a million questions like a crazy person. Hehehe . . . Thank you for giving me your thoughtful opinions! You are the best!

To Erisy and Rowan, my babies. You both were excellent taste testers throughout the book writing process and I hope you grow to love cooking as much as I do! My dream for you, once you're old enough to cook, is to make some of these family recipes together. Your Ông Ngoại would be so proud and Mommy loves you so much!!!

Last but not least, Nate: You are the reason this book is here, the reason *Honeysuckle* exists, the reason for everything our life has become. You encouraged me from the day we met to do what I love and to dream big because life is too short to be sitting in a cubicle hating my job. We were two bored kids when we uploaded that first video to YouTube and I never thought it could turn into what it is or where we are today. Who knew this would become our business, our career?! Thanks for making my dream of having a "cooking show" come true. You never let me settle and you inspire me in every way. This book was truly a labor of love and you contributed not only to the storytelling and design but to the dreaded physical labor of cleaning the kitchen and putting away the dishes every single day. It did not go unnoticed. I never was good at cleaning and am so thankful you're always there to lend a helping hand. We've come so far since our days on Alma Street, haven't we? I'm lucky to have you as my *Honeysuckle* partner and as my husband. I love you so much.

INDEX

ABOUT THE AUTHOR

Honeysuckle is a food and lifestyle channel hosted by Dzung Lewis, whose dedication to simplifying gourmet recipes and lifestyle design has allowed her to grow into a YouTube star. Dzung has been cooking since she was eight years old, when her grandmother taught her authentic Vietnamese recipes with a twist. Her exceptional content, produced with a playful edge, has made her channel a destination with a full-video production business, which she runs with her business partner and husband, Nate. Her mission is to "inspire young women across the globe to use food and lifestyle choices to develop creativity, self-confidence, and community in everyday life." She has worked with *Bon Appétit,* Target, Google, Starbucks, and other major lifestyle and food brands. She and Nate live in Los Angeles with their daughter, Erisy; son, Rowan; and border collie, Ollie.

Copyright © 2020 by Dzung Lewis

Photographs copyright © 2020 by Eva Kolenko

All rights reserved.

Published in the United States by Rodale Books, an imprint of Random House, a division of Penguin Random House LLC, New York.

rodalebooks.com

RODALE and the Plant colophon are registered trademarks of Penguin Random House LLC.

Library of Congress Cataloging-in-Publication Data

Names: Lewis, Dzung, author. | Thomson, Jess, other.

Title: The Honeysuckle cookbook : 100 healthy, feel-good recipes to live deliciously / Dzung Lewis, with Jess Thomson.

Description: First edition. | New York : Rodale Books, an imprint of Random House, a division of Penguin Random House LLC, [2020] | Includes index.

Identifiers: LCCN 2019049037 (print) | LCCN 2019049038 (ebook) | ISBN 9780593135600 (hardcover) | ISBN 9780593135617 (epub)

Subjects: LCSH: Cooking, Asian. | Cooking, Vietnamese. | Quick and easy cooking. | LCGFT: Cookbooks.

Classification: LCC TX724.5.A1 L49 2020 (print) | LCC TX724.5.A1 (ebook) | DDC 641.595--dc23

LC record available at https://lccn.loc .gov/2019049037

LC ebook record available at https://lccn .loc.gov/2019049038

ISBN 978-0-593-13560-0

Ebook ISBN 978-0-593-13561-7

Printed in China

Book and cover design by Stephanie Huntwork

Cover photographs by Eva Kolenko

10 9 8 7 6 5 4 3 2 1

First Edition